Changing C

Changing Churches
Building bridges in
local mission

JEANNE HINTON

CHURCHES TOGETHER
IN BRITAIN AND IRELAND

Churches Together in Britain and Ireland
Inter-Church House,
35–41 Lower Marsh
London SE1 7SA
Tel. +44 (0) 20 7523 2121; Fax +44 (0) 20 7928 0010
info@ctbi.org.uk or (team)@ctbi.org.uk
www.ctbi.org.uk

ISBN 0 85169 264 8

Published 2002 by Churches Together in Britain and Ireland

Produced by Church House Publishing

Further copies available from CTBI Publications, 31 Great Smith Street, London SW1P 3BN Tel: +44 (0) 20 7898 1300; Fax: +44 (0) 20 7898 1305; orders@ctbi.org.uk www.chbookshop.co.uk

Cover designed by Church House Publishing

Typeset in 10.5 on 13pt Palatino by Vitaset, Paddock Wood, Kent

Printed by Creative Print and Design Group, Ebbw Vale, Wales

Contents

Contents

Foreword

At a time when traditional church institutions are eroding, how are Christians at the grassroots responding to the challenge of change? Is there new hope coming from below? How can local churches re-engage with their neighbourhoods in a plural society? What is effective Christian witness today?

These are some of the questions behind Jeanne Hinton's down-to-earth account of a journey across England, Scotland, Ireland and Wales to look at the evidence. Hers is a story of practical questions and everyday realities, of travels and tales which explore the very meaning of 'church' today.

Starting from the daily experiences and struggles of Christians as far apart as Luton and Llansantffraid, Jeanne met congregations and Christian initiatives of every shape and hue. Their stories are vivid, touching, realistic – sometimes painful and often surprising. What they have in common is that they were all part of a three-year ecumenical learning experiment which formed the second stage of Building Bridges of Hope (BBH).

BBH is not another quick-fix programme for church renewal. Neither does it claim to be an instant recipe for evangelism or community building. Rather, Building Bridges of Hope is an invitation to create long-term commitment, to seek regular accompaniment, to welcome constructive criticism, to look at how each aspect of the church's life fits into a wider whole, to seek God's presence in the world, not just the church.

Through Jeanne Hinton's travels – in the people she met and the stories she heard – we get a flavour of what difference this makes in practice. Gifts differing and vulnerabilities faced turn out to be very much part of God's life-giving purposes. Jesus Christ lives with us in the everyday, not in some remote 'religious' ghetto. Ordinary situations, says the author, are the material of extraordinary possibilities.

This book is therefore a story of great encouragement for local churches. You do not have to be big, glamorous or special to see the gospel of love come alive in everyday situations – but you do have to be prepared to persist. You can stay loyal to the insights of your tradition and denomination, but you also have to be open and change.

Our churches, in spite of the rumours, are far from dead. But if they are to navigate the future – to take the timeless message of God's transforming love in Jesus Christ into a rapidly changing environment – they will have to look, feel and act very differently.

Simon Barrow
Secretary, Churches' Commission on Mission,
Churches Together in Britain and Ireland

Feast of the Epiphany, 2002

Acknowledgements

I would like to thank all those who responded so warmly to the idea of this book and who welcomed and shared so generously with me, and drew me into their enthusiasm and vision for a 'new way of being church'. In particular I would like to thank the Hope Community – Anne Marie and Sue Allen in particular – for giving me a base in the West Midlands, and the Johnstone family (Martin, Sue, Robbie and David), for similarly sharing their home with me on journeys further north.

I am grateful too to the folk at St Barnabas, Stoke, Plymouth, for agreeing to my including a memory of a previous visit in this book, and to Tony Barker, minister of Zion Baptist Church in Cambridge for allowing me to edit his account of their story, published previously in a New Way booklet. My thanks too to Ruth Harvey, Editor of the Coracle and a member of the BBH's 'new forms of church group'. She kindly read a draft manuscript and made invaluable suggetions. Ron Ram's galvanising role in Stage B of BBH should also be noted.

CCOM and I very much appreciate the endeavours of Sarah Roberts at Church House Publishing for expediting an impossible schedule, and would also like to thank Kate Hughes for her thoughtful copy-editing.

Perhaps most of all I am grateful to Simon Barrow and others within the Churches' Commission on Mission/Building Bridges of Hope who suggested I researched and wrote this book. It has strengthened my belief in the important contribution of BBH to a changing church. I have been encouraged, challenged and I think a bit changed by the journey. That can be uncomfortable, but I am grateful nevertheless!

Jeanne Hinton

Introduction

I write this at the end of my journeys and now reflect how different this introduction would have been if I had written it three months ago, before I set out. I have some different perceptions now; others have been deepened and affirmed. I have met and talked with many different people, and these encounters have warmed, challenged and changed me. I am immensely grateful to all who welcomed and shared so openly with me. The journeys that follow are almost all about people taking risks – tentative steps, often quite small to begin with – in response to the tug of the Spirit of God.

The background to these journeys was an invitation from Building Bridges of Hope (BBH) to journey to a number of places where participating congregations and others* had engaged in the first stage of BBH. BBH is a 'living laboratory', working with churches locally and nationally to discover 'best practice' for moving from maintenance to mission. Stage A was a consultation phase on both European, national and local level. Stage B accompanied, observed and researched about 40 local places over a three-year period as they tried to move from maintenance to mission. These are the partners referred to throughout and they were supported by observers with a careful framework of questions. In Stage C, which started in 2001, the seven key factors learnt from Stage B will be explored in a wider but more focused context, as a number of existing 'pilot' initiatives test ideas, support initiatives, challenge institutions and break barriers. (For more detailed information on BBH, see Appendix 1 on p. 129.)

Up to this point my connection with BBH had been as a member of the 'new forms of church' sub-group; my knowledge of the overall process was a bit sketchy. That was all to the good because it meant that I was making a genuine journey of exploration: mostly I did not know what I would find. I deliberately did not read or reread background papers and reports on Stage B until all the journeys had been completed and written up. I brought to this reflective task, however, a number of parallel experiences, in particular as a member of a network called New Way and as a contact person for the European Collective of Basic Christian Communities. New Way seeks to promote a new way of being church, primarily through small community formation. The European Collective is a network of basic Christian communities that came into being in the 1980s – a parallel development to basic ecclesial communities in Latin America and elsewhere in the world – which is also a 'new way of being church'. There are so many threads to this tapestry of the Spirit's weaving.

One of the words that surfaced regularly in our 'new forms of church' sub-group was the word *yearning*. It also came to mind often on my journeys and was an undercurrent to many conversations. In the sub-group we travelled and met with different groups engaged in different praxis. We discovered a great yearning for relationship, for meaning and purpose, for honesty and authenticity, for justice and freedom, for community. Above all, for authenticity: a desire to deepen one's experience of God in a way that is life-giving and relevant to the world in which we live. Travelling again, I have discovered this same yearning among all those I met – in congregations, new forms, value sharing groups. The yearning is not confined to any one group or expression of church; again, it is a bubbling up of the Spirit both within the mainstream and on the edges.

Indeed the bubbling is broader than this, as the use of the word *soul* indicates. Soul as a word is no longer the prerogative of organized religion. It has almost become a secular word and is perhaps viewed with some suspicion for that reason. But its broad usage today is indicative of a widespread spiritual search across all sections of society. At a health spa I pick up a magazine and it opens at a page on 'Secrets to wellbeing'. Inspiration, perception, awareness, soul, faith, growth, change: these words permeate the article. 'It's usually your body you want to change, but what about your soul?' the author asks. In their well-publicized research (*Understanding the Spirituality of People who Don't Go to Church*, Nottingham, 2000), David Hay and Kate Hunt tell us that more than 76 per cent of the national population admit to having had a spiritual or religious experience. An important challenge came to me from these journeys: Where are the places within the Christian tradition where this soul hunger can be explored in a totally non-judging way? Where are the places and spaces that can easily be found and where the doors are not locked? There are a number in the pages that follow. A prior step, however, is learning to listen to what lies behind these secular explorations into meaning and spirituality. We have to learn again the language of the soul. We have to listen to the undercurrents, to the heartbeat – God's heartbeat.

In all this I am aware how limited this book is, how much is not represented. We would have liked it to be more representative. Some visits I hoped to make didn't work out. There are very obvious gaps – fewer groups of an evangelical persuasion than might otherwise be the case, no black-led churches (though a prominent example from Sheffield was part of Stage B), few from suburban or affluent areas. However, I am confident from journeys made at other times that this yearning of which I write touches all sections of both the church and society. My hope is that in reading about these journeys you will listen for the undercurrents, the heartbeats. For here is the energy, the passion, needed for change.

*Note: The 'others' include, crucially, experimental situations which we describe as 'new forms of church', and church–community partnerships where Christian values are put to work alongside the values of different communities. The latter were part of the 'values sharing' sub-project.

First journey

Having agreed – gladly – to take on this task of visiting and writing and producing a manuscript within four months, I then realized what I'd agreed to! I decided then and there that the only way to meet this deadline was to write as I went along, I knew also that I would have to pace myself; the idea behind this book was not only to share stories but to reflect on them as well, and that takes time. So I decided to make three journeys and on each of them to find a base from which I could make mostly day visits and then return to write up the visit the following day. It was a good decision and has worked well for me.

On my first journey in May 2001 I based myself in a house in Kent belonging to an aunt who had recently moved to Wales. The familiarity of my surroundings eased me into the schedule I had made for myself. From here I travelled to Folkingham, a rural Church of England parish in Lincolnshire, and two days later to an area in Luton which is 80 per cent non-Christian, to the Beech Hill Methodist Church which has a sizeable West Indian membership. Here too in Luton I visited a café – or was it a church? Also Grassroots, a programme supporting and enabling new initiatives in Luton and elsewhere. I had hoped to visit Zion Baptist Church in Cambridge, but this was not possible, so I picked it up later on in the four journeys.

A lot gathered for two days travel !

1

Building community in Lincolnshire

Considering the short notice I had given, I was not surprised that the Rector, Canon Hall Speers, was not able to see me the week I wanted to visit Folkingham. It was Jill Morris, a lay member of the church, who rang to arrange a day for me to visit and chat with her about Building Bridges of Hope. I was impressed with this emphasis on lay leadership, so much in keeping with the grassroots ethos of BBH.

Folkingham is a long way from a train station, a 'retired' market town buried in the heart of rural Lincolnshire; the nearest large town is Grantham. Jill met my train at Peterborough, a 25-mile drive, so we had plenty of time to talk. The previous Saturday Jill had represented the church at one of the get-togethers of the newly formed Association of Building Bridges Churches. She spoke about the change she sensed had taken place over the past year in a number of the churches represented there: 'It seems almost everybody now has a story to tell about engagement with their local community', including her own church.

As we travelled Jill talked about Folkingham and the nearby villages included in South Lafford parish; 12 churches in all. 'Hall is responsible for all twelve. He is also rural dean which means he has oversight of some 30 others. At the moment there is a shortage of clergy throughout the deanery, so he helps out where he can. We do have a curate but he is leaving and may not be replaced. You see why he couldn't manage to see you!' she commented. She then went on to tell me about an initiative she and others in the parish had started a while back, to make sure that there will always be a Rector for the South Lafford parish. The trigger was a report that the Church Commissioners were about to cut back drastically on the number of clergy in rural areas. 'They changed their mind, but we went ahead anyway', Jill said, and now a number of fund-raising activities are held each year to maintain a clergy fund. Lay leadership was obviously well in place at St Andrew's, Folkingham, and throughout the South Lafford parish, but the possibility of going it alone without a clergyperson is not one they want to entertain. I felt we would come back to this conversation later.

The Pop-In Club

In recent years Folkingham, like other villages locally, has been the focus of considerable social change. Building development has increased the population of the village by 50 per cent, from 400 to 650. This in a village that until 1981 had remained much as it had been pre-war, except for a few new post-war 'Wimpeys'. Earlier it had been a small, self-sufficient community, with 90 per cent of its working population engaged in agriculture.

Now it is more of a dormitory town, its inhabitants mostly retired or commuting to work elsewhere. This is a hard situation for older 'locals' to adapt to and seemingly makes it difficult to re-establish any sense of community. Nevertheless the attempt is being made and one place where it is happening is in the South Lafford Pop-In Club.

The Pop-In Club meets every Monday, from 10 am to 3 pm. A new venture, it had only met twice before my visit. When Jill and I arrived, some thirty or so folk were already settled in, clustered around a chess game, dominoes, a half-finished jigsaw, and handiwork. Most of these pursuits seemed incidental: conversation hummed.

It was easy for me to slip in and be part of one of these groups. Most people thought I must be a newcomer to the village and laughed to think I had come all the way from Poole in Dorset.

What surprised me was that the first six people I talked to had all moved to the village within the past year or eighteen months. Living in a small village myself I knew the anxious response to the thought of newcomers: 'They won't want to get involved', 'It will destroy what community there still is.' Certainly here in Folkingham that was proving to be a false assumption. Indeed, it seemed to be the newcomers who were bringing the community to life again.

It was a while before I met anyone who had lived in Folkingham for twenty years or more; one lady had been born there. 'In those days you knew everyone,' she told me, 'it took a long time to do your shopping, always stopping to chat.' Now, however, she too is glad of the Pop-In Club as a place to meet others. There seemed to be a remarkable cross-section of the community among the forty or so in the village hall: many retired people, some very elderly, but also a cluster of younger mums; a spread of ages as well as a social mix, and men and women in fairly equal numbers. I checked that out with Jill's husband Alan, who I discovered was active in the community in a variety of ways. 'Yes,' he told me, 'it's pretty representative and that's good.' I sat for a while with the women busy with tapestry squares depicting scenes from the life of the villages. A visit to the city of Wells had inspired this idea and the collage will hang eventually in St Andrew's Church. Conversation turned to how to regenerate local communities. 'The pace of life nowadays is hard to beat', said Jane. 'I think most people want to be part of a local community but don't have the time to do anything about it. It's those who are retired or the unemployed or mums who are at home looking after the kids who are the potential community builders.'

Those who come to the club for whatever length of time contribute 50p, which also pays for a simple lunch. About a dozen stayed for lunch and saying grace reminded us that this is a church initiative. There had been quite some discussion about whether or not to do this, but everyone seemed to take it in their stride. I discovered that Tom sitting opposite me was not a churchgoer, although he appreciated that churches were good places for people to meet. 'I like it here,' he told me, 'there are always good stories to hear', which reminded me of the laughter earlier on at the table where he sat with three other men, an untouched jigsaw in front of them. He had a good story to tell me himself: he had met his second wife Peggy in North London at a club similar to the Pop-In; they had taken up an offer by Virgin Airlines to fly to Miami and be married on the beach there. He was such a neat, retiring kind of man that I was a bit taken aback, but it was a good illustration of his point about good stories to hear.

After lunch I sat again with the busy sewing group, mostly younger women, some of them struggling to thread tapestry needles. 'Not used to this at all', one told me, but the activity helped us all to sit comfortably together. The conversation became a bit more serious at this point, mainly about the effect of the foot and mouth crisis on local farmers and also weather patterns. Jane herself is a farmer; she and her husband work a small arable farm and it was the weather that had affected them this winter, causing considerable damage to crops. We talked about the stress brought about by these crises, and that here was a role for the church. Jane went and found leaflets for me about the Lincolnshire Rural Stress Network, which local churches support. Later we talked about the Rogation Day Service to take place in her village that coming Sunday. This time it would have to be held on church ground because it was not possible to walk the parish boundaries as they usually did. She hoped that more non-churchgoers might come this year; the need for prayer was apparent.

The Pop-In Club was not the result of a lot of planning; it kind of happened. For eight or nine years Monday evening at Jill and Alan Morris's home was open house; people came and brought their sewing or knitting, and 'we all had a jolly good natter'. Jill and a few others also went to an upholstery class in the village, and there was dismay when this had to close. Jill wondered if it could be reconvened at their home and Monday made an open house all day. She and Alan talked about this and then decided it was impracticable – 'too many tacks and pieces of thread everywhere'. The ball was rolling, however, and the impetus now was to look for another location. 'And once we took it out of the home an obvious question was why keep it just a small group?' said Jill 'There are many people who are desperately lonely, particularly elderly and widowed and single mums.' The way the Pop-In Club has been organized is very simple. Responsibility is shared among eight people, two sharing the organization for any one day. The ethos is the same – things to do and mostly as an excuse for a good old natter. Homely.

On the phone Jill had told me that the Pop-In Club had resulted from their involvement with Building Bridges of Hope. When later she told me the actual story, I couldn't quite see the connection. Her answer was interesting. 'I think becoming part of Building Bridges helped us to think differently about things. It changed how we see things; our focus if you like. Things followed from that.' I liked that answer. It is obvious that the process has been useful, although the results are not always easy to pin down. Building Bridges is not after 'results' as such; it is more concerned with observing and facilitating reflection. Jill commented that the Pop-In Club might have happened anyway but probably not in quite in the same way: 'I might not have said "This ought to be a church project rather than a community project".' She laughed when I wondered if the same kind of reflection was continuing without a participant observer coming regularly, and said: 'Not really, we're all running around like headless chickens!' A stewardship campaign was to start soon, however, and she felt that would help to correct the imbalance; it too would focus on the church's mission. A good bit of analysis had gone on naturally during the day, perhaps because I was there.

I had a question for Jill. I wondered if connecting more closely with the community had brought about any changes to the regular services, in particular the liturgy.

She felt that any such changes would be strongly resisted, but once a month there was a Praise Service led by lay people, which was more informal. 'But,' she added, 'that's changing too. As lay people we're not very confident about doing any preaching; we really need the clergy.' Alan later commented that he felt church services needed to relate far more closely to people's real lives.

In the afternoon Jill and I walked down to the church, an imposing tall-towered medieval building, an integral part of this attractive village with its old coaching inn and many fine houses. Inside, this fourteenth-century church feels welcoming and its decorative style, including the trefoiled arches of the fine chancel screen, is a reminder that this building also has historic value. It is not difficult to understand why there is a strong desire to keep such buildings open, but how helpful are they to the present mission of the church, I wondered. I discussed this later with Jill and Alan. 'An important thing, I think,' said Alan, 'is using the church for things other than services.' In recent years, concerts had proved popular. 'The church is a focal point in the village. It is important to find ways to attract people into the building. That is a start.'

I was still concerned about the pressures on Hall Speers, knowing that these are repeated in many rural churches across Lincolnshire and elsewhere in the country. Some change in the patterns of ministry seems crucial. Jill told a story about suggesting that she, rather than the Rector, should visit a certain parishioner. 'Why would I want you to call?' was the somewhat offensive answer. In some country areas change can come hard. 'But the economics may force it upon us', says Alan, and even with their ministry support scheme they know that to be true.

2

More than a meeting place: Luton's Café 2000

'This is like a church...', 'This is a church too...'. In our short conversation Jean had repeated this conviction three times.

'Because it's a place where people meet together, find a welcome...?' I was probing, wondering what she meant.

'No, not just that!' Jean was quite emphatic. 'There's a feeling about the place.'

It's something quite special – more than just a meeting place. There's something...'

She paused.

'Spiritual?' I wondered.

'That's it,' she said, 'like a church.'

We laughed and I asked her if she went to church herself. 'No!' she said. We laughed again.

We were sitting talking over a simple meal of pasta and salad. Tables had been bunched together down one side of the room, so that twenty or more of us sat down to a communal meal. Jean and I sat opposite each other, lingering over the end of our meal. To one side two elderly West Indian women had finished their meal and returned to their patchwork. A Chilean woman I had practised my Spanish on during the meal collected plates and cups from the table. Across from us a local Methodist minister sat in earnest conversation with David Cowling from Grassroots, a support group (see p. 18). Further down the room three washing machines were in frequent use. There was a hum about the place, an ease, it felt comfortable to be there. Through the window I could glimpse the somewhat bleaker shopping precinct of Marsh Farm. Step outside Café 2000 into this precinct and the warmth, the hum, vanished; you shivered, and not just from the wind blowing through. But inside Café 2000 the atmosphere was different; this was not like any church I had ever belonged to, and yet…

Café 2000 started when a group of local women began to meet once a week at the local library. At first they had nothing in mind apart from a time to meet together for support, but as they talked they realized they all knew other women struggling with the harsh realities of life on the Marsh Farm estate. When a unit became available in the shopping precinct, they took the plunge and rented it. With the help of grants, they opened the unit as a community café, primarily a place for people to meet. At the start the café had three aspects: the café itself, the small launderette and secondhand clothing for sale. I had visited the café before when it was called Rags and Roses and secondhand clothes filled the window space, but a local survey revealed that many people did not like the idea of clothes and food being together in the same place and so the clothes went. Café 2000 was the new name.

I overheard a scrap of conversation: 'Hilda said the other day she wanted to go back to Jamaica. "Leave us?" I said, surprised. "No, no, but I would love to start a project like this back in Jamaica".' This said a lot. Café 2000 is more than a café to those who come regularly. It is not a club either, anyone can come through the door and feel welcomed. Those who come have created an informal community, or perhaps several communities. Early morning a group of mums after dropping their offspring at school and sit in a group of comfy chairs, drink coffee and chat. Others come later, stay for lunch and then drift away to make room for others. What was apparent was that all those I met 'owned' Café 2000 in some way; it was 'their place'. There are 'managers' and 'volunteers' but the roles are not immediately apparent, and when I thought I had it sussed out I found I had not. Café 2000 is also aware that there are those in the community who cannot or would not come even to a community café. Jean and Mary were later going to visit some of the housebound.

I had joked earlier with Mary about her unusual necklace of house keys and a whistle. 'Dog whistle', she told me. She had sat most of the time at the end of the stretch of tables, picking up and putting down her sewing in a dilatory kind of way. Mostly she just sat, but as Jean told me, 'Mary is one of those who is always there for any neighbour in need.' It was Mary who drew my attention to the collage hanging on the wall; I kept going back to look at it and soon realized that it summed up for me the uniqueness of this Café 2000 community.

Each piece of the collage was about meaning: what was important, what gave life. Each individual piece spoke of that; collectively it drew these 'meanings' together.

There were repeated themes: family was one, but others, more strikingly, were dogs and family pets. Mary's 'piece' spoke of the importance to her of the local football club.

Charles, a young, tall, striking West Indian, had contributed a more reflective piece in bright blues and greens: grass, trees, a pond. 'You get a different perspective from such space', he told me. Jesus was part and parcel of all this too, a worked parable, and Ann had started on a square that had the imprints of feet turned in to make a circle: 'They're Buddhist feet', she told me. They were also symbolic of her interest in circle dancing. She was about to add a candle and an eye, a symbol of Muslim belief. 'I'm a Christian,' she told me, 'but I want this to be inter-faith.'

'Given the connections you make with church,' I had said to Jean during our conversation, 'do you see the possibility of having some simple liturgies – little services – here in the café that would enable deeper reflection on what life is about, here on Marsh Farm?' Again her answer was immediate, 'No, it would not work here.' She went on to say that anything so formal would immediately scare off most of those who felt at ease coming to the café. 'Many just wouldn't come any more, but to sit and talk about such things when they naturally arise, that's different', she concluded.

The collage seemed to me a natural way to spark just such conversations, and in its way it was also sacramental. Words on one piece of the collage read:

> Here is a place where all are welcome
> from every place and denomination
> all we need is communication.
> So open up your hearts
> and listen now
> it won't be long
> we must stand strong.
> So life is a test and must go on
> fight on Marsh Farm.
> For soon the time will come
> when the Marsh Farm spirit
> will be one
> and everything we dreamt
> is not just a vision
> but reality.

The café's creed.

The collage had only just been begun; the first pieces had been hung to make the place look brighter and more interesting to another visitor. The day before, Deputy Prime Minister John Prescott had called, visiting Marsh Farm to campaign in the run up to the general election. Over the next ten years Marsh Farm will receive 50 million pounds of regeneration money, part of Labour's New Deal for 'most needy' communities, and Café 2000 will benefit from this. In time Marsh Farm will not be such a bleak place. An 'administrative unit' has already been opened further along the shopping precinct from Café 2000. Officials came to open it and to say exactly how it should be run, but 'That's not the way we do it here', Jean had told them. Jean and others involved hope that the unit will become a place where local people feel welcome and 'own' the New Deal and help shape its outworking for the local community.

'Another church?' I joked. 'Yes', said Jean; we laughed, but we both knew there was an underlying seriousness to our laughter. My visit to Café 2000 had given me a lot to ponder.

3

Resurrection in Luton: Beech Hill Methodist Church

The next story I heard was about a church that almost gave up.

Ten years ago Beech Hill Methodist Church in Luton had reached a low point; membership had dropped, the congregation was ageing, the area had changed its character, the building needed restoring. Perhaps it was time for the church to close, but the situation needed to be assessed before such a drastic step could be taken. The church already had a relationship with Grassroots – David Cowling, its founder, is a Methodist lay worker – and it was to Grassroots that the church turned for help. A series of weekends was initiated when members came together to appraise, reflect and decide on the church's future. At the end of this period it seemed possible that the church could make a continuing contribution in Beech Hill.

That moment of seeing new possibilities was the beginning of a fresh start. A lot of hard work was needed to follow it up – hard work and the need to sustain belief in the vision that came out of those weekends. A Grassroots mission partner from Brazil, Reynaldo Leao, came to work part-time at the church and brought with him new perspectives. 'His infectious enthusiasm and the way he made everyone feel their contribution was important kept things on track', I was told. Leao encouraged the church to undertake a survey of its immediate locality, and in particular to find out what local people wanted to see happen in their community. Health and fitness centres topped the list of local needs, together with meeting facilities and a place for young people to meet. The church now had to consider whether any of these needs could help to shape its future.

It was at this point that Building Bridges of Hope asked the church to take part in Stage B. They agreed and from that point Bob Weir, a participant observer, visited regularly. The questions he asked provided a regular review on how things were going. He also brought with him stories of what other churches across the country were doing, some of them in a similar situation. Now, five years on, there is no longer any talk of closure. There is still apprehension about the future, but also evident excitement at embarking on a new challenge. The old decaying building is to come down and in its place a complex of buildings will accommodate homes for the frail and elderly, a meeting space for community activities and a worship place. Beech Hill Methodist Church is situated on a busy main road and is well-placed to offer facilities to the local community. What is important is that the new buildings contribute to the life of the area and are seen as relevant. 'We cannot be sure we've got it right, but we hope so', was one comment.

I met with five lay members of the congregation and asked about some of the factors that had enabled change to take place. All strongly asserted that it was not one but a number of factors that had worked together to take them forward. The pressing need for costly repairs to the building, a growing sense of the church's distance from the community, Grassroots being just down the road and able to pitch in, Building Bridges approaching them when it did – all of these had been contributory factors and everything had come together at the right time.

The process had brought about one fundamental change in how they as members saw themselves and their role. 'I think we were classic cases. We expected the Minister to do pretty well everything, and that's how it mostly worked.' When they had a new minister a few years back who had worked abroad and did things differently, their complacency had been knocked. 'He did not expect to do everything. It was a different style indeed.' For a year they were without a minister at all – another strong contributory factor to change. A new perception of what being church means has taken place – or is taking place. The membership of Beech Hill Methodist Church is 75 per cent Caribbean. The five I met were all British and white. 'Our Caribbean members prefer not to take on church responsibilities themselves.' This opened up another area I would have liked us to consider in greater depth, but there was no time.

Soon, as a church, they will lose their building. That is already viewed with a kind of nervous anticipation and will perhaps be the biggest challenge yet. 'I suppose we will meet in our home in small groups?' was an anxious response. There was a difference of opinion among the five about whether there was the skill and experience among them to lead such small groups. However this is going to be handled, it will obviously set a style for the church in its new worship space.

Beech Hill has now agreed to engage with Stage C of Building Bridges of Hope, as part of a wider ecumenical venture. Its focus is on 'sharing faith'. 'This is often a rather neglected area', David Cowling commented. 'Discovering how best to engage with the local community is one thing, but is that to be all? There is a great need to discover how faith can be shared, and not least in a multi-faith context.' 'Over the years those left at Beech Hill Methodist Church have felt themselves engulfed by waves of newcomers from different cultures and also faiths', Julia Dowding, the new minister at Beech Hill, told me. 'As nearly always happens in this situation, you turn in on yourselves. The challenge is to find the strength to move out into the community and be able to offer a welcome to those just arrived.' The newer arrivals are from Asia, a threat to those who came earlier from the Caribbean and have found churches like Beech Hill a safe retreat. 'But,' says Julia, 'those who are already settled are in a position to welcome others, and to do so is empowering.'

The decision not to retreat but to engage in a new thing in complex and diverse surroundings has many ongoing ramifications. Signs of life.

4

Supporting change: Grassroots

Grassroots is an initiative that brings together global insights from south and north. Its contribution to the processes of change among churches in Luton is considerable. That it is available locally to offer resources to Beech Hill Methodist Church and other congregations and also to Café 2000 and similar 'new forms of church' is a result of a decision taken by Grassroots a few years ago to change its direction. David Cowling, its founder, explained this to me.

'When we started out, a lot of our work was done through conducting workshops around the country. What we discovered was that those who came caught a renewed vision, but got bogged down back in their own situations. Change takes place slowly over a long period of time, and resources are needed on the spot to help sustain enthusiasm and vision. When we realized that, we decided to cut back on the work and to root ourselves locally. We contribute to what is happening here in Luton and are learning ourselves from being part of something which is real and ongoing.'

'Grassroots has greater freedom to watch for the new thing because it is not so encumbered with baggage from the past', reads its Annual Report 2000. Seeing things in a different way or from a new perspective is essential to this watching 'for a new thing', and this is where Grassroots' mission partners come in. Over the past ten years these have come from many different parts of the world to share in this watching process with others.

One practical way that this has worked out recently has been through the 'Rediscovering the Bible Project' facilitated by Pamela, a mission partner from Brazil. This took place in an Anglican parish in Hitchin: three cycles of six weeks' group Bible study over a one-year period. At times the learning process touched on controversial issues; practically, it challenged deeply held understandings of mission. Controversial maybe, but the methodology is now being taken up by other nearby parishes as well as further afield.

In Hitchin the learning process was sharpened through the inclusion of people with disabilities in each group; this in itself brought a different perspective, and the process will be ongoing in the Anglican church there. Those who previously felt that they did not have enough formal biblical and theological knowledge to take on leadership of the groups have discovered that they do have skills and experience to offer. In line with Grasssroots' decision to root itself locally, Pamela writes that 'real sustainable change is more likely to take place through long term work at grassroots level'. During her time here in the UK her work in the parish was the priority.

The gradual process of coming to see things from a different perspective can be hastened by relating to partners from other countries and cultures. 'That's a start,' says David, 'but every day we meet those who are different from us, certainly here in Luton. The greatest challenge is to be open to listen to those among whom we live and to the most marginalized in our communities.' Here David sees the potential for a greater learning relationship between the local churches and initiatives such as Café 2000. Both would gain from this: Café 2000 is continually in need of encouragement and support.

Shanti Hettiarachchi is a Grassroots partner from Sri Lanka who has been working with the organization for the past five years. 'In inter-faith dialogue,' he commented, 'it is difficult to hear the other person unless you believe that he or she has truth to offer you, a revelation. God's truth is so vast, are we Christians the only ones to hold it? It is not just a matter of openness to other faiths, but to all people we meet. Unbelievers, partial believers, might they not hold some truth, some perspective that is a gift to us? A gift of the Spirit?'

This comes back to David's comments about present confusions with regard to sharing faith. In response to a proposal from Grassroots, the local council of churches in Luton has agreed to take part in Stage C of BBH. Its particular area of exploration will be sharing faith: exploring ways to share yearnings, values, aspirations and faith in relation to the gospel story beyond church circles and to do so in respectful and creative ways.

5

Reflections: Ministry

Jill Morris's comment about the change she perceived among those congregations represented at the Association of Building Bridges Churches has stayed with me. The change has to do with moving out into the community, illustrated by what I have written about the Pop-In Club and Beech Hill Methodist Church. Café 2000 has things to say about this too. I know that as I visit others over these next few months, I will be learning more about this aspect. I am encouraged by it, but...

The 'but' comes from an anxiety that this often difficult step of moving out is perhaps not so difficult – not as difficult as acting on new perceptions about ministry or the liturgy or the use of church buildings. Unless new forms and new ways are found here, it is possible that deeper involvement in the community will never realize its potential to 'be church': it may be in the community, but to 'be church' in the community is another matter. That is something to be explored on this journey.

The area of 'ministry' is the one I have been thinking about most from these visits.

Not so much from the angle of a rural dean struggling against the odds to oversee some forty little churches, but from the lack of confidence expressed by lay people in both places that I visited. Not a lack of confidence about taking on 'service' in the community, but about engaging in ministry – leading services or Bible study groups. Most conversations I hear about 'ministry' have to do with 'ordained ministry'; lay training has increased but does not have the same priority. Perhaps we should turn that on its head.

I remember a conversation with the Principal of a theological college in Sao Paolo, Brazil. I asked him what kind of courses they had at the college – a fairly innocuous question, but I have never forgotten his reply.

'First,' he said, 'we have courses for trade union leaders, Secondly, courses for leaders of small Christian communities. Thirdly, for clergy. Fourthly, for bishops.'

The priorities that are clear here were borne out at the gathering of Brazilian basic ecclesial communities (CEBs) that I was attending. The 70 bishops present were all in casual dress, but I spotted them as those 'who listened', and invariably I had identified them correctly. Here the priority was a laity trained for both social and church spheres and a clergy who enabled and supported. The lay facilitators at the gathering, mostly young women and men from small rural communities, were confident and articulate in their handling both of groups and the Bible. A situation that still exists in many parts of Latin America despite the difficulties CEBs have encountered from a conservative backlash.

That is the situation in Brazil, where change was born out of crises in the 60s and 70s. The day before I travelled to Folkingham, I watched the BBC's *Countryfile*. The programme focused on the crisis in Cumbria and the devastation caused there by the outbreaks of foot and mouth. Those who spoke on the programme were certain that the style of farming in Cumbria will have been changed for ever by the crisis. They spoke of a move away from intensive farming to organic development run on cooperative lines. What I have written of my visits so far shows factors that make for change, but it is never just one factor, but several, and among them the importance of being enabled to see things differently. But a sense of real crisis? I'm not sure. Where will the compulsion for real change come from?

Second journey

June, and I made my way to Wolverhampton and to the Hope Community where I was basing myself for the coming ten days. These surroundings were already familiar to me and I could learn about recent developments in the community while staying here. When the community agreed to be a participating congregation, it was based in several apartment blocks on the Heath Town estate, with two Sisters 'working to improve family and community life'. There have been changes since, and I write about these changes in two parts – at the start and the end of my visit to Heath Town.

From Heath Town I made daily trips: to the Welsh borders to encounter a remarkable crossing of denominational borders; to Leeds to hear about a different kind of ecumenism, a making-community between settled and unsettled people; and to Leyland where a Catholic church engaged in parish renewal is at the heart of another ecumenical endeavour. Indeed, most of the stories seem to be about a working ecumenism. The common factor.

6

A place of Hope:
Sisters in Wolverhampton

Heath Town is a 1960s housing estate near Wolverhampton town centre. It is also where the Hope Community is based, one of the participating congregations. Over the years I have made several visits to the community. Once, early on, I took a taxi from the station. The taxi driver had a worried look on his face when I told him where I wanted to go, because Heath Town had a rather dubious reputation in those days; drugs and gang warfare prevailed. Once on the estate, I wanted to be dropped and find my own way, which would be easier on foot than directing a nervous taxi driver, but he absolutely refused to drop me and only did so when I told him to take me to the community centre where, I assured him, I was known. It wasn't where I wanted to go, but still it was kind of him to be so solicitous.

That was ten or so years ago. Heath Town is a very different place now. 'A nice place to live', as I was told recently. Indeed, it is sometimes so quiet that it is uncannily like my small quiet village in Dorset. However, it comes to life at times, after school hours and at night when the noise of cars revving and voices calling continues well after midnight. It is a mixture of high rise blocks, maisonettes and a handful of terraced houses, although families no longer live in the high rise blocks, which are now considered a risk for children. In time there is talk of other changes: demolishing some properties and building new housing, retaining and refurbishing what is sustainable. That will cost a lot of money and is a long way off. But the changes that have already taken place have made a difference.

In front of the block where I am now staying is a large grassed area landscaped with shrubs and trees, a place for children to play and adults to idle and talk. Previously the area was hemmed in with a high tower block; there was no space and nowhere to play. Now there is also a large floodlit playing field and a sports club. This is the exterior face of change. The biggest changes have come from residents discovering they can have a say in what happens here. That is where the Hope Community and others have come in.

The story began when three Sisters of the Infant Jesus (usually known as the IJs) were asked by the local Roman Catholic church to conduct a census on the Heath Town estate. They began going from house to house, notebooks in hand, climbing long flights of graffiti-marked stairs or risking the small lifts, which were claustrophobic and more often than not smelt of urine. But whereas the outside of the estate was much as they expected, the people they met were not so predictable. The three Sisters found that there was a warm welcome for them – as religious sisters. They were invited in, offered tea and told confidences. The stories told were of struggle and injustice, of weariness and a lack of hope. The census forms were almost abandoned; the Sisters stayed and listened. It was this experience that led them to ask, 'Why aren't we living here?'

The council were happy to make two flats available and the Sisters moved in. They had moved to *be* there, not to do or to evangelize. They waited to see what kind of life would emerge, what the Spirit would do. An invitation to a Tupperware party had a knock-on effect: they asked for the next one to be at one of their flats, and once people knew where the Sisters lived, they came. An open house was established and became a springboard for much of the action that would take place on the estate in the following years. Action by residents successfully campaigning for the closure of a local company emitting lead, for a bridge linking two parts of the estate to be reopened, and for other positive changes to take place.

My first visit to the community was in 1991. I went back several times after that and things became familiar to me. I felt at home. I enjoyed the bustle in the flats (increased to four by now), the conversation, the coming and going. If the sisters were out visiting, I was more than happy to answer the doorbell and offer a welcome and a cup of tea. In the morning particularly, three or four residents would turn up: 'nothing else to do'. Once or twice a week in the evenings a number gathered, sometimes for Faith Alive – lively conversations about life and faith and informal prayer. It was often out of these times of relating the Bible to life that action on the estate followed. One Bible passage that is often recalled is the one where Nathanael first meets Jesus, 'the son of Joseph from Nazareth'. 'Can any good come from such a place as Nazareth?' Nathanael asks in disbelief, a challenge indeed to those living in a modern-day Nazareth. Staying in the community during that period was demanding, but you kind of got drawn in. Things have changed radically in the intervening years, and not just on the estate. The familiar has disappeared; something else has taken its place.

Staying here again I realize that I am struggling to adapt to this change, even resenting it a bit! The focus for the Hope Community is no longer those flats (now again reduced to two) but a centre in the shopping precinct. I have two weeks based here as I visit other congregations and communities – time to learn about the changes.

7

A new ecumenism: Llansantffraid ym Mechain

The Welsh Presbyterians were without a minister, the Catholics without a building. These situations were fraught with frustration for both parties, but then became a catalyst for 'changing church' in the Welsh border villages of Llansantffraid ym Mechain and Llanfechain.

Llansantffraid ym Mechain is a fair-sized village of around 1200 inhabitants; Llanfechain is smaller, around 600. They are set in the green fields and rounded hills of the two border counties, Montgomeryshire and Shropshire; farming country. Together the villages have six chapels (Welsh and English Presbyterian, Welsh Wesleyan Methodist and English Methodist), two Anglican parish churches and no Catholic church. The nearest Catholic church is in Welshpool, some distance away. There are more chapels than churches, but fewer chapel members overall and some of the chapels have no ministers. This situation caused the Welsh Presbyterians to set the ball rolling in 1990 when they approached the Church in Wales minister, then Llewellyn (Lyn) Rogers, and invited him to be a minister in their new experimental 'community ministry' in Llanfechain. To Lyn Rogers that request came both as a 'little miracle' and a huge privilege. Significantly, the invitation came from the denomination itself, not just the chapel. This arrangement and later developments began to remove the centuries' old culture of distrust and ignorance that had existed between church and chapel.

The morning I arrived at Llansantffraid Rectory I was greeted by Jennie, Ern and Michael from the Church in Wales; Gloria, a Welsh Wesleyan Methodist; and Shirley, a Catholic. Michael Bennett is now the Church of Wales minister for the two villages; the others are all lay members of their churches. The conversation turned almost immediately to the place of the chapel in Welsh village life. It stirred a personal memory: I was born in South Wales, but the family moved to England when I was two. 'We're chapel, you see', my parents told me on a number of occasions when I asked why we did not go 'to church' as a family. I was in my teens when I first went into a C of E church, and it was some time before I persuaded my parents to do so too. This morning's conversation reinforced for me the huge gap that has existed historically between chapel and church, a gap that combines not only religious differences or persuasions but cultural and political ones as well. In both myth and experience, the chapel carries the 'welshness' and 'church', the seeming arrogance of the English. Disestablishment has helped Welsh Anglicanism, but suspicion and ignorance die hard. The memory of both was present in the room as we all talked.

The Catholics had never had a church in either village. As elsewhere, their parishes are widespread and the nearest church (building) in Welshpool. 'A long way to go', said Shirley. Now local Catholics worship every Sunday at St Garmon's, the Anglican church in Llanfechain. When Jennie and I visited that church later in the day she showed me two candles standing on the table – or altar. Ordinary white candles, no adornment; but turn them round and on the other side there is the impress of the cross in red and black. Simplicity for the Anglicans, adornment for the Catholics: a wonderful arrangement, accepting and economical. The organist is a Catholic and plays for both services. Things have changed – wonderfully!

The changes began when the hall used as a mass centre was unexpectedly pulled down. Fr Gerard approached the Anglicans to see if they could help. The request opened up a myriad of questions, issues and practical considerations. It meant the Anglicans having to change the times of their own services to make dual use of the church possible. In the end it necessitated taking 'a leap in the dark'. Lyn Rogers has since written:

> We learned that at the heart of the unity of the Body of Christ is the paradox enshrined in Bethlehem, Calvary and the gospel, that apparent loss and the willingness to lose in love, is the gateway to a new life. The miracle is that we found that same understanding of the gospel in each other and realized it, only when we took that leap.

Here again it seems that many different factors brought about change. One factor that cannot be disregarded is the personalities and gifts of particular people. Gloria told a simple story that illustrates this well. She was at a fête and literally bumped into a cheerful looking man who greeted her with warmth. She immediately felt drawn to him, and then discovered that he was the local Roman Catholic priest. He became a friend and changed her perception of Catholicism. Lyn Rogers similarly brought a personal charisma: his commitment and vision contributed to change happening. Building bridges was a dream he had pursued long before Building Bridges of Hope entered the scene. When approached about BBH, there was an immediate interest. 'I think we were getting a little comfortable', Lyn has commented. 'BBH enlivened, sharpened and enabled us to think more deeply about what we were doing.' It has been the means of drawing together a small group to reflect on developments, and this has provided a crucial 'place of safeness' to explore the theological, ecclesiogical and socio-logical implications of change. All those groups listed above – chapels and churches – are represented in this group.

A situation 'in which the English language dominates and where there is need to relate more to Welsh culture', I had read before coming to Llansantffraid. Early on in the conversation Shirley had said: 'This is the context for all that has happened here.' All nodded, but it became obvious that it was hard for them to be explicit about what this actually meant. There was some ambivalence about how essential an issue the Welsh language was for them as a group. Here on the Welsh borders the issue of language was perhaps not so sharp, they said, as in other parts, further north. Mixing English and Welsh cultures and language has a long history here, howbeit often turbulent and painful. Mixed with the ambivalence that morning was mutual deference: they were two sides of the same coin. They realized this and spoke about it openly. 'Language is really not that important an issue after all', Welsh-speaking Gloria says to Jennie. 'No, but it is important', Jennie – the incomer — replies. There was appreciation of the fact that Michael always gives communion in Welsh to those whose first language is Welsh. 'I know a little Welsh, enough', said Michael. Somehow they knew they were not quite grasping the nettle on this one. What concerned Michael was that the culture should be valued and maintained. What I appreciated in a new way is the fact that the chapels are indeed guardians of language and culture. I understood too in a new way the place of the actual buildings in the Welsh countryside; an integral part.

The increasing demise of Welsh chapels is indeed a sad occurrence. I learnt that one chapel would have to close because of new health and safety regulations – no loo! Jenny and I passed this chapel later; its rich red weathered brick and the small paned windows with their flaking white paint bespoke a long life. A corollary to this is that I learnt the regulations do not yet apply to the Anglican churches listed as part of the national heritage, and so not to the two local Anglican churches. It was impossible to get away from the seeming discrepancies – or injustices – that this little group is bravely working with. But something new is taking shape in the middle of it all.

This was all very well but perhaps a bit insular. What effect was this new ecumenism having outside the churches, on the local community? There was a bit of a silence here. Interest has been stirred when meetings or events have taken place outside the church building – in the local community centre, for instance.

There was quite a crowd for the showing of the BBH video, because the two villages had featured strongly in it. There had been open air events planned for the spring and summer this year, but foot and mouth regulations had put a stop to these. Mostly, however, there was a group consensus that 'the time was not quite right yet; they had a long way to go still'. All the denominations might be represented on the 'building group', but representation can often mask the actual situation. There was tacit agreement that there was not a lot of interest in what had or might happen beyond this; the enthusiasts were being allowed to get on with it.

'It will take time to get everyone on board, and then we will be ready for the next step', said Gloria. Jennie had a different angle. Some time back she had either heard or read of the 'sleeping dragon' – Welsh spirituality buried but stirring. We were back to this again, the current underlying the whole of our conversation in one way or another: 'A restlessness in Wales.' Something brooding, indeed?

8

People at Home in Leeds

I last saw Eileen Carroll some years ago; she was leaning out of a window of her bedsit and pointing to a row of small houses further down the street. 'I have a dream', she said. The dream was of establishing a small community of 'settled' and 'unsettled' folk living in close proximity to each other. Her dream of a house has come true but, as so often happens, the dream has changed in the process. Eileen is a member of a religious congregation, the Sisters of Charity. When I first met her in 1994 she, with others, had already spent a few years in Leeds trying to form this new kind of community which had, at its heart, people familiar with homelessness and alcoholism.

There are so many strands that led to the beginning of the group which became known as PATH; the initials stand for People AT Home. Pivotal was a conference on homelessness organized by Faith in Leeds in 1989. Eileen had been working with homeless people in Leeds for some time and was asked to lead a workshop at the conference. She declined, but responded to the invitation to bring some of the men she had got to know with her to the conference. Three came. The day did not start out well – registration meant writing names in a book, and John couldn't write ('I've forgotten my glasses', he said). 'No Smoking' notices faced them everywhere. Those who had come with Eileen obviously felt as uncomfortable as she did. 'Never again', she thought, but then in a smaller group a conversation began about 'what it was like to be on the other side of the door'. A clergyman present described how someone had come looking for sandwiches just as his wife had collapsed and he was trying to call an ambulance. Things got lively at that point – and interesting. When asked by the organizers to report back, the group was short and to the point: 'We want to meet again.'

That beginning led to the formation of the PATH group, which met once a week. There was to be no 'them' and 'us', no 'doing for'. A simple structure developed for the weekly meetings and in time a workshop came into being and icons, toys and wooden household objects were made. These were sold to raise money for chosen charities, with a small amount kept to buy more materials. From the beginning no attempt was made to raise money for the group's own needs, nor to look for grants; the group was to be self-supporting.

Outings became popular and also short holidays. The first period of time spent away as a group was at Worth Abbey in Surrey (Benedictines) and the monastic atmosphere seemed to make a deep impression. The Guest Master commented that the visit from the PATH group had been a privilege for the monastery too: 'We can too easily get caught up in our own affairs and lose sight of the deeper realities of life.' A surprising comment, perhaps; who was teaching who about the deeper realities?

I spent the best part of a week in Leeds in 1994, most of the time with PATH. I remember the funerals I attended, three in one week. The lifespan of those who are homeless and alcohol dependent is invariably short, but their life is remembered by their peers. Funerals and opportunities to grieve are important and taken seriously. Those who come, men and women, are always respectfully dressed for the occasion. I remember Taffy, who took me in hand and looked after me in what was for me unfamiliar territory. Visiting Eileen this August I learnt that Taffy too is seriously ill – in his early fifties. I also remembered how proud those who belonged to PATH were of their membership. Too proud perhaps, because in time they wanted to keep out those they considered 'undesirable', a battle between the 'druggies' and the 'alkies'. I remembered too a PATH evening when, towards the end of the evening, we sat in a circle ('a gathering time'). Notices and news items were shared and at the end we sang a song based on words provided by Callum, one of the men, in response to a remark that 'we need a decent song that's our own'.

> We're on a path from loneliness to friendship,
> It isn't easy and the way is dark and long.
> We try to love, respect and help each other,
> And as we go, we sing our Pathway song:
> Let's keep right on till the pathway ends,
> Just trying to be a circle of friends,
> Wherever we go, wherever we roam,
> Let's never forget we're People AT Home.

The evening usually ended with a song, a prayer or a reading – something reflective. Psalm 36 was adapted as the PATH prayer:

> We believe, Lord, that you guide our steps
> And make safe our path.
> We believe that even if we stumble we shall not fall
> Because you love us and hold us by the hand.

This was not used at every meeting, but when requested. Experiencing this 'gathering time' I was impressed at how easy everyone seemed to be with the transition from games (snooker) and chat to conversation and prayer and back again to general activity and clearing up. Perhaps, I thought, an unsettled life makes one adaptable and also reflective about life. Eileen herself believes that people whose lives are precarious, chaotic and often without boundaries appreciate some form of structure and pattern if it is not rigidly imposed.

As a visitor I was made to feel at home too. A difficulty was that PATH itself really had no home: in five years it had moved five times. Some premises were ideal, some less so, and this was a strain that took its toll in time. There were other problems as well. Numbers of people, young and old, came over these years to be part of what was still a very loose-knit community. From the start they tried not to have 'helper' and 'helped'. All had to take responsibility and jobs were shared out equally, but some 'unsettled' folk became too protective, while some of the 'settled' became too particular. 'When it got to endless discussions over whether we had skimmed or semi-skimmed milk, I knew I had had enough', said Eileen. Eventually, when it became necessary in 1996 to look yet again for other premises in which to meet, Eileen called it a day and stepped back to have a good think.

Eileen and PATH had always had a lot of support not just from her congregation but from a network of local churches and secular organizations, people to whom Eileen could turn for advice and support. For seven years she had been living in a bedsit too small to invite others into. 'What I really want is a place where people can just come and make themselves at home', she told her Provincial Superior. She was authorized to go ahead and look for such a place, and a friendly local councillor helped her to find what was needed – a ground floor flat in an old Georgian house. It has two rooms, kitchen and bathroom, a garden back and front, and a big cellar that serves as a workroom and meeting space. (It now also houses blankets and clothing collected by the Simon Community for their weekly soup run, in which Eileen participates.) The house is near the city centre in a quiet cul-de-sac just off a busy bus route. Above all it is a place of peace and quiet – a bolt hole – for Tom and Joe, two of the men I met, and for many others who are regular visitors. The occupant of the top flat is a 92-year-old woman who is delighted to be welcomed into this 'community of sorts'.

Eileen uses the smaller room as a bedsit and the larger front room is for communal activities. She is wonderfully creative at arranging spaces that work – tidy but not too tidy. On Wednesday and Thursday she, or someone else, is always at home. These two days are the 'hinges' around which everything else turns, although people may be invited to come at other times by arrangement, according to personal need or work to be done. There is one golden rule: those 'in drink' must wait until they have sobered up before coming in. Kingston Terrace is much more than a drop-in centre; it is pre-eminently a place where those who come can find peace and quiet and also privacy. Numbers are necessarily small, so that people can become known. Down in the cellar is a kind of deep alcove which the men are trying to make damp-proof. Eileen told me that Tom had said to her one day, 'If we put a curtain at the entrance, then if someone wanted to have a bit of a cry, he could go in there.' I too thought it would make an ideal chapel. 'Perhaps in time it will be', said Eileen. 'I'm just waiting for the right moment.'

There are no specific or formal 'prayer' times at Kingston Road. It is all definitely less organized than in the old days of the weekly PATH meetings. On the other hand, Eileen has more opportunities to respond to anyone who wants to go 'further' or 'deeper' into what is 'real'. Six of the men and Eileen had just come back from three days at Mount St Bernard monastery. By always using the term 'the men', I am following Eileen's usage. She is not satisfied with this term but cannot find any other. To speak of 'the homeless' hardly honours the relationships that exist. Better still is to be known by name: 'Often we are sitting in this room with its large window overlooking the front garden and gate, and someone will jump up and call "Here's Frank", or "Here's Tom". To be greeted by name is to be given dignity.'

'Will any of the monks talk to us?' Frank had asked early on in the visit to Mount St Bernard. One elderly monk had come and talked about life in the monastery and the meaning of the monastic vocation, Afterwards most of the men went to talk to him individually, to be listened to, taken seriously, absolved and reassured. David, aged forty, barred from all the day centres and shelters in Leeds because of his violence in drink asked if there was 'Owt he could do to help'. One of the monks asked him if he had ever used an axe. 'Yes, in prison', came the reply. David then spent the best part of two days chopping and stacking logs, slipping away now and then to sit quietly at the back of the church for the singing of the Offices.

Prayer at Kingston Terrace takes a number of different forms. Music is important. Eileen has a large collection of cassettes and finds that most of the men love listening to music:

'It opens deeper dimensions'. 'Many have been put off somehow by "church" as generally experienced. I try to encourage the innate response to beauty and to quietness. In this way prayer does not have to be formal.' Sometimes a candle is lit, there is a short time of silence and John or Joe or another friend is remembered. Some Taizé music recently evoked a response from Francis: 'That was lovely, that was. Would you write down the words for me, please?' The words were 'My peace I leave you, my peace I give you. Trouble not your hearts.'

The phrase 'a new form of church' was used several times by Eileen in our latest conversation. How did all this connect with more formal church structures, I wanted to know. Eileen's reply was immediate, spoken with conviction. Neither Kingston Terrace, nor PATH before it, could exist without the support of the church as institution. Both – the new and the old forms – have gifts to offer to each other. What was important was creating networks of goodwill whereby both learn from and support the other.

Eileen has been pivotal to this story. I remembered the conversations about leadership we had way back in the PATH days – whether consensus worked, whether some dominated. How did Eileen feel about this now? She responded characteristically by telling me a story. She had come to Leeds originally at a time of searching in her own life and, at the request of her Provincial Superior, to gather information about possible ministry among homeless people in Leeds. Eileen did what she was asked and found she was drawn to this ministry herself. She told the Provincial this when she reported back and then discovered that her response had been hoped for. Her Provincial had seen in Eileen a gift Eileen was unaware of herself, a charism or calling. 'That's leadership,' Eileen commented, 'discovering and encouraging the gifts we see in each other.'

She can see these gifts in the men who come to Kingston Terrace. As I left, Joe called us aside to see the crazy-paving he was laying around the little pond dug a year ago. Tom was perched precariously up a ladder trimming the hedge. Kingston Terrace was obviously their place too; they were taking a pride in it. Earlier on they had welcomed me as if to their own home, which in part it is, though they do not live there. Miss Heath, the 92-year-old, was just returning from the day centre. As she made her slow progress up the garden path with the help of her white stick, I could see how delighted she was at the welcome she received.

Eileen is realistic about the fact that not everyone is called to live the way she does; in fact it is the few who are. She lives very simply and her home is shared with many others. She knows she could not do this without the support of her congregation, nor without the support and friendship of many within local churches and organizations. There are also those who cannot comprehend what she is about. But she is adamant that she cannot and will not be some 'token person' standing in for others. 'My job', she said, 'is continually to feed into the body of the church. The challenge and the calling is to the whole church.'

Before Eileen went to Leeds she had met a man named Frank who was looking in vain for a church where he would be welcomed, Eileen wrote then:

> If there isn't a church for Frank to go to, could there be a church that would go to Frank? Could there be a church that would enter his own very real life, speak his language, offer him a sense of belonging, not just to a settled group of friendly people, but to a body of pilgrims, on a journey? Could there be a community that would help him express what is going on in the world, enable him to get in touch with his deepest longings, assure him of forgiveness, renew, uplift and draw him beyond himself?

Not long after writing that, Eileen was beginning to see that 'it is not only people like Frank who need the church, but that the church needs people like Frank.'

9

Partnership in Mission in Leyland

'Here we are ten different churches with ten different views. The big question has been how to bring everyone together.'

A renewal programme taken up by the Catholic church of St Mary's, Leyland, has led to 'building bridges of hope' across the ecumenical divide and also out into the community. The day I visited Leyland I was able to participate in a meeting of the 'Building Bridges of Hope' group, attended by representatives from the Catholics, Anglicans and Methodists, with apologies that evening from the URCs (the Baptist church at the moment does not take part in this initiative, nor do the house churches or fellowships). The evening was much more than a meeting of representatives; it was a gathering of friends. 'Having the time to get to know one another; that is what is important.' This taking time has paid off and I was moved by the quality of relating, the care and respect, that were present. Twice, different people spoke of having been moved to tears by the depth of feeling present on previous occasions. Here were people discovering each other across different traditions and, most importantly, as people together.

'Leyland is stronger religiously than many other places in England', Jonathan Cotton, the parish priest, had told me earlier. Ironically, disputes between Catholics and Anglicans going back to the 40s may have contributed to this religious sense. Whatever the reason, there is an openness in the town to the churches, a pool of goodwill which is increasing as the growing unity among the churches in Leyland becomes apparent. Leyland has a population of 27,000 and a relatively low level of unemployment compared to other areas. A lot of light industries have now replaced the former established ones: pizzas instead of lorries and trucks. Trucks are still produced, but not in the same quantity, while Leyland is now one of the largest exporters of pizzas to all parts of Europe. However, the town is not affluent. Walking just a few streets from St Michael's church revealed some of the disparities in the town; 'There are quite poor areas here too', as I was told that evening.

Jonathan Cotton came to St Mary's with a background of involvement in Catholic lay movements, particularly Focolare. 'A very practical experience of sharing with other people. Indeed, my whole life and experience has been that. A living out of the gospel and a sharing with other people in the name of Christ.' There had been a gap of six months between Jon's coming and his predecessor leaving. The parish pastoral council had been strengthened during this period to take on more responsibility and this led to participation in a diocesan parish renewal programme, Partnership in Mission. The most helpful part of this again had to do with the parish pastoral council, its role and relationship with the wider body of church and community, and this also helped to define a new relationship between priests and people; 'a real call to conversion ... to building new ways of relating and working together'.

'Many priests already understand their role in this way and express this in their ministry. However, others feel threatened by the new demands or ill-equipped to fulfil them. Some express willingness but prove unable to recognize the full implications or to change their basic attitudes' (a quotation from the Partnership in Mission training manual). To me it was obvious that Jonathan had already moved a long way along this path.

It was at this juncture, soon after Jonathan's appointment, that Building Bridges of Hope approached St Mary's to ask if the church would participate in BBH. 'They needed a Catholic church and we were willing!' It was a bit of a laid-back start, but Jon is now an ardent advocate of BBH and his enthusiasm has spread beyond his own parish. BBH and the parish renewal programme ran in parallel, with Ron Ram as the participant observer appearing from time to time to take his 'snapshots'. 'That gave us a focus in a different way, and it was this that really awakened us to mission.'

By the time I joined the BBH group for their evening meeting, Stage B was in the past, but the momentum continues. '"The Word was made flesh..." Here I find an emphasis that gives equal importance to the social gospel as to the spiritual.' Alan Stone, a Methodist lay reader, had started the evening with a short reflection on John 1:1-14. One of their tasks as a group, he emphasized, was to convince other members of their churches of this biblical truth. Conversation throughout the evening showed that everyone faced this problem of a wariness of 'social gospel' from other members.

Together we watched the *Bridges to Build* video, and this was fascinating, not least because of the many exclamations of 'Ah! That's so and so' and 'Do you remember her?' Interaction between differing BBH groups during Stage B had resulted in a lot of positive interaction and a sense of bonding that was also present in the small Leyland group. We then split up into three groups to discuss set questions from the booklet accompanying the video. I joined a group discussing

> Where in the life of your community or workplace do you see signs of God's presence and purpose (name and unnamed as such)?

As a group we were quick to name such signs; they came easily to mind. This led on to a question about the need to help others to recognize God in these 'signs'. Some people thought we should not be too anxious about this. There was a story about Jonathan going on his bike to a photographer's shop. He stayed around and chatted for a while and as he left the owner said, 'You don't care who you talk to, do you?' and followed this up with: 'You know you lot do a lot of good in this town.' Was such recognition enough? This was a question that wasn't going to go away and indeed we returned to it later in the evening. We talked about making regular services more accessible and relevant to non-churchgoers, something close to my heart. This issue is going to be around for a while too!

It is possible that the BBH group will soon have a definite public face in the town. A project is under way to open a charity shop to raise money to fund and support community involvement. This will also be a public face of the churches together in Leyland. Different churches are already involved in running community concerns, with an increasing level of support now from others. One scheme receives and passes on gifts of furniture. Another, Tools for Reliance, receives gifts of tools which are then 'fettled up' and sent to third world countries. In Leyland there is no lack of those with engineering skills who are good at doing the 'fettling'. A third is a rent guarantee scheme – guaranteeing the first month's rent to anyone unable to find it. There is also a move now for the local churches to enter into the various community forums. 'If one of us is present, then we are all present' is the ecumenical intention here.

'I've always been interested', Jon told me, 'in this whole idea of letting Christ live in us, of sharing with others – with other churches and also those outside the churches – and experiencing living together our unity in the name of Christ. Jesus when he was alive didn't thrust religion down people's throats. He simply pointed to our humanity, what was truly human, godly. He related as a person and gave himself as a person and through that came our redemption. To my mind that is what BBH is about – it's not pushing a particular kind of church. In the BBH groups there are all kinds of experience and theological persuasion, but we all ascribe to this gospel priority.'

Jon continued, 'I've experienced the power of the presence of God's love – well, love really – and it has changed me, but how to share that with others is extremely difficult. I see BBH as helping me put into effect what I would like to do anyway – to work alongside others who have the same values. I guess I'm saying that in all these ways BBH is a kind of gift of the Spirit.'

10

The Hope Community revisited

Sue Allen, who is manager of the Hope Family Centre, came to the estate in 1993. She was then, she says, 'anxious and withdrawn'; this was not the place she wanted to come to. One day a member of the Hope Community called and that changed things around. Sue has been a part of the Community ever since and involved in all its struggles and dreams. A mother of four, she is a calm maternal presence around the place.

The identifiable face of the Hope Community is now the Family Centre on the shopping precinct in the heart of the estate. 'It is important to be visible.' There are still two flats in the maisonettes, but there are no Sisters living there now. Anne Marie spends two nights a week at No. 122 and there is still a bed for visitors at No. 120. Perhaps these too will go in time. On this visit I stayed at No. 120, but for most of the time I was the sole resident of both flats. I have been glad of the opportunity to adjust to the changes and appreciate them. Actually, what feels new to me is not so new: a family centre was the dream that emerged several years back and plans were drawn up, but a funding application failed. The dream came about another way when changes to the estate made it possible for the present Family Centre to open in 1999.

A walkway leads to the shopping precinct. The first time I saw the Family Centre it kind of took my breath away: bright, open, airy, it gives a wonderful lift to an otherwise still grey precinct. Cheerful painted sunflowers on the windows and the bright colours of the toys and play areas seen inside beckon you in. The building adjoins another and there is one reception area for both the Family Centre and the Estate Management Board. This arrangement is one that Sue Allen worked for: 'The Hope Community's calling has always been for all people on the estate, not for families only. Our closeness continues this link but in a different way.' Some of the accommodation is shared – kitchen, committee and conference rooms, computer workshop.

The shared building adds immensely to the improvements to the shopping precinct. A few years back there was little to draw one; most of the shops were closed and boarded up. Now a few are opening up again. The community hoped at one time to have a café as part of the Family Centre but health and safety regulations precluded this. They were also aware of a need for a crèche on the estate, but realized that they were not the ones to provide this. Other people are coming and supplying some of these needs, and that, says Sue, is definitely preferable. Despite changes, the estate still suffers from a bad image: newcomers arrive with its old reputation in mind, one-third of the properties change hands every year, and those who come are often themselves struggling with a low self-image. It is a vicious circle.

At one time the Hope Community was a prime mover – and often a provider; now I could see that it works in partnership with many others, and I found this exciting. What is important is the Hope Community's charism of a welcome to all. Underlying this is the belief that God is to be found in every person, and often what is needed is just to uncover that seed of faith. Margaret Walsh, one of the first Sisters who came to live on the estate, is fond of saying that they came to plant seeds and discovered that God had already done the planting. Alongside the play area in the the Family Centre is a chapel. There was discussion about having it somewhere less prominent, but it was decided that it was important for it to be in the centre of activities, accessible for any who want to use it. Staff and volunteers meet there regularly for prayer; children meet for a Bible class and are encouraged to talk about their experiences and express them through art and play; Bible and life connected here too. At the flats Anne-Marie meets regularly with a small 'p and q' group, which stands for peace and quiet – the thing that is most wanted by those who come. While I was there a group of eight went off in the Hope Community minibus for a two-day retreat at a centre in Wales. The sharing of faith is something that happens quietly, almost incidentally, but it happens.

The Hope Community was identified by BBH as 'a congregation'. It is a congregation with a difference. There is no formal membership, but for the some 100–150 people who attend the regular 'Celebrations' it 'is their way of being church'. Once a month in past years and several times a year still, Community Celebrations are held in the Community Centre. These are faith celebrations and people on the estate always both plan and lead the event. There are plans for the next Celebration to take place in the precinct itself and to be a big cultural event. Heath Town is a reception area for asylum seekers, who now make up 10 per cent of the estate, and they will be invited to help plan the event, celebrate faith and cook a variety of different foods. Unusually perhaps, there has not been any friction caused by the arrival of these newcomers. 'Heath Town has always been a very accepting, welcoming place', Sue told me. Perhaps one of those God-seeds which have been uncovered.

11

Reflections: Enabling and empowering

At the Hope Community Eilish and I washed the dishes together and – as in my first journey reflections – the topic of our conversation was change. A different angle this time. We continued talking, propping up the wall in the small kitchen. I confessed to my struggles with the changes that had taken place in the community, changes that I nevertheless recognized as positive. We talked about the difficulty that institutions and churches often have in adapting to change. But this does not always happen. Eilish told me that the IJs now have a different approach to their mission. Whereas previously Sisters might expect to spend all their working lives in one situation – abroad or at home – now they are prepared for short-term placements only and the emphasis is on enabling and empowering local people to take on the project or initiative themselves. The Hope Community is a good example of this approach.

The conversation had come about because I had commented on the rapid change happening in 'new forms of church', in contrast to the slow pace of change evident within the congregations I had visited. Rapid change in 'new forms' comes from responding to change in local communities; a lack of 'baggage' makes possible what is often problematic in local churches. An ability to adapt to change, however, seems essential.

Eilish had put her finger on another essential: the emphasis on enabling others points to new models of ministry and leadership. Three, if not four, of the stories in this journey point to this. What comes to the fore is the importance of recognizing and affirming a variety of gifts, especially gifts of leadership. The Church of the Saviour in Washington DC, for example, has pioneered a new way of being church built around recognition of members' gifts and charisms. Gordon Cosby, the minister, became aware of the rich diversity of gifts and interests in his congregation. Some had teaching gifts, some were artists, some musicians, others had the idea of running a coffee house and so on. On the premise that people do best when something is stirring deeply within, he encouraged the growth of small mission groups around these interests. A new structure gradually came into being of small faith communities engaged in mission tasks. In time many of these grew to be small church communities still linked but each with its own identity. To enable the growth it was necessary from the start to evolve a whole new pattern of training to support this development; there were no models to draw on. This is an exciting concept of how to support engagement in the world.

This is all about seeing people as central to God's mission: their stories, lives, concerns and struggles, people in all their humanness. While I was on this second journey I read in a report some words of the Dalai Lama: 'We must strive to see the humanness in the other.' These words well-expressed what I had been encountering in my visits. Often it is the human encounter that makes the bridge, as Gloria recounted in the story of Llansantffraid. This is about what is small, simple, often undervalued. It is about taking small steps to connect with people in their ordinary, everyday lives. Again and again I have been heartened to hear about what has grown from such small steps. Any congregation, anybody, can do it.

Then there are such wonderful surprises! It is a delightful surprise to hear of a man whose life is wholly unsettled finding consolation in the very settled ambience of a Catholic monastery. The fact that places and times of peace and quiet are so important to many today – to many different categories of people – is surely indicative of a wider interest in spirituality than often thought. It points too to a whole variety of ways by which church can be expressed in a neighbourhood or workplace or in the home. This again calls for a variety of different gifts to enable it to happen.

Connecting faith to everyday life is what first drew me a number of years back, to learn more about the basic ecclesial communities in Latin America. In the first flush of enthuasium I saw the same spawning of communities happening here. 'It couldn't, you know', a friend who is an episcopal priest told me. He went on to explain that for churches to impact local neighbourhoods in similar ways here would need cooperation at least between the different denominations – an ecumenical advance not evident then. On these first two journeys I have been impressed by the growing strength of ecumenical partnerships in the places visited, and the resulting impact locally. Here indeed is hope.

Third journey

I had to rearrange this third journey. When I returned to Heath Town in June, after my overnight stay in Leyland, I had some sad news. My aunt whose house I had stayed in on my first journey had died suddenly and unexpectedly that day. She was someone close to me, important to me. That was one time when I didn't write up the story the following day. Instead I went straight to Cardiff where she had died. On the train I wondered whether I would be able to complete this book at all. There would be much to do, funeral arrangements to make and, anyway, would I feel like it? Now later, starting my third journey, I realize that I am quite glad to have a job to do, and equally glad to have a nearby park where I can walk and feel my feelings.

The park was close to where I stayed near Glasgow with Martin and Sue Johnstone and their two young boys, Robbie and David. They gave over their fair-sized dining room to me, my laptop and all my papers and allowed me come and go as I wished. I was glad of their support and the opportunity to talk things over with Martin. My first day I flew to Belfast! Here I had another overnight stay and a myriad of impressions and challenges of what it is like to be 'church' astride Belfast's peace line. Other visits were nearer – to Motherwell to see a venture I had heard a lot about but never visited, to lunch with members of an alternative worship group near Glasgow city centre, and then on to Edinburgh to hear about that city's club scene and 'creating spaces'. Then a day visit to Teesside again to hear about emerging networks of goodwill – signs of God's kingdom..

On the way south again, struggling with my ever increasing load of papers and books and my heavy laptop, I called in at Sheffield to visit The Furnival. On the way there I thought I could well have done with going straight home, but I was wrong. The Furnival was not to be missed. It was another ecumenical venture – a church in a pub – 'seeking to be a Christ-like presence intimately linked with the surrounding local community' as the BBH booklet states. By this time I thought I had seen it all, but no – surprise is the word I use in telling this story,

It was of course good to get back home too, and to have time to reflect at greater length on all I had experienced.

12

Finding common ground in Belfast

Springfield Road Methodist Church is a church that ended up on the wrong side of the wall. Indeed, whether it likes it or not it is a part of the wall that straddles loyalist and republican areas in West Belfast. When the so-called 'Peace Line' was erected, houses, schools and whatever stood on the spot inevitably became a part of the improvised wall, with concrete and steel fencing plugging the gaps in between. A few yards down the road from the church is one of the massive iron gates that mostly remain open to allow traffic and pedestrians through, but can be closed in an emergency. If such an emergency occurred during a church service, members could only get back home by taking a long journey around another way. It was one of many dilemmas for a church struggling to exist in an area known worldwide as an epicentre of Northern Ireland's 'troubles': the nationalist/republican Falls area on one side of the road, loyalist Shankill Road on the other. As I shall recount later, their answer to this dilemma was typically positive and creative.

The church was 'planted' on the Springfield Road by Belfast Central Mission in the 1920s. The area was then (predominantly) a Protestant area, and the congregation a growing one: the building was large enough to accommodate a congregation of 400 and more. From the 60s on, as the situation in Northern Ireland deteriorated, the area surrounding the church changed its character. A growing Catholic community led many Protestants to move out, and an escalating situation of suspicion and distrust grew up between the two communities. In the 70s, with the situation now out of control, the

'Peace Line' was erected. Springfield Road Methodist Church was left with a dwindling congregation and a building too large and too expensive to keep up; it was a low moment indeed for the remaining members. It was hard for many of them at that time to think about more than mere survival. However, the then minister, Gary Mason, saw the possibilities in the situation. The problem of the closed gate in the wall pointed among other things to a way forward.

Gary discussed with the Methodist Superintendent, David Kerr, the possibility of the church buying the two adjoining small terraced houses, which were on the other side of the wall. From the garden of these two houses there was a gate next to the church car park which gave access to the Protestant Shankill area. There were not many would-be tenants wanting to move into that area. 'I'm thinking of buying two houses in the Shankill', David Kerr told a neighbour, who looked at him in some amazement. 'And I have a tenant for you,' he said. 'It was a moment of surprise, a God-moment. The tenant he had in mind was a Catholic nun, Sister Noreen Christian.

At that time Noreen was living as a member of the Cornerstone Community further up the Springfield Road. The Cornerstone Community evolved out of a cross-community prayer group, the Clonard Prayer Group. Those who belong to it, Protestant and Catholic Christians, live and/or work locally and are committed to working for reconciliation between the two polarized communities. Some live in the Community House, which is also a place of meeting and activity. The symbolic value of their being together is important to them. In the early 90s Noreen began to feel the need for a second ecumenical presence in the area, this time on the Protestant side of the line, on the Shankill. Her hunch matched Gary Mason's – the timing of the Spirit.

When Noreen moved into the new home in the Shankill, volunteer workers moved with her, a succession of them over the years. The houses are right alongside the huge iron gate that dominates that part of the wall. I found its towering presence hugely intimidating, but step inside Noreen's house and you walk through one room into a large airy conservatory and outside into a garden full of space and colour. Here one can breathe again, and along the top of the wall itself Noreen has also planted a vine which immediately changes the character of the wall. All of these things help in a situation that otherwise feels so wearily impossible. They have named this house and community, The Currach. The Currach is a boat from Celtic times, small but sturdy. The vulnerability of this little craft symbolizes their own, a vulnerability that comes from the choice to live on the peace line.

The Currach Community is, like Cornerstone, an ecumenical community whose members come to live together for at least a year, seeking to build and support healthy relationships with each other and with the surrounding community on both sides of the interface. Exploring appropriate ways of praying together is another focus, and other projects have developed with women's groups and with children. Every Tuesday, in response to requests, The Currach offers a 'reflection space' for individuals and groups active in the community. The proximity of the Springfield Methodist Church to Cornerstone and The Currach prompted a further creative move. The church building was underused and in bad need of repair; Cornerstone and The Currach had limited space for developing projects.

Gary Mason suggested combining their various interests and developing the church premises as an inter-community space. This was eventually agreed to, a partnership was formed and work began on renovating the premises. A fourth partner also joined in the venture, the Mid Springfield Community Association (MISCA), a secular community group. MISCA has since ceased to exist but some of it programmes continue. The new purpose-built premises, with a dedicated 'church' space, was opened in 1996 and the project was named Forthspring. The river Forth runs close by and there is a spring reputedly near the building.

Forthspring brings to mind other images, such as a spring of life. If the renovation of their building for use in the community was heartening for at least some church members, it also brought further heartache. In the past years there have been four arson attacks on the building and in particular the church itself has suffered. David Campton, who has succeeded Gary Mason as minister, showed me the scorch marks still visible on a charred baptismal font and a fragile cross made of lace which had survived intact when much else had not. Again it is a symbol and such symbols are important, but sometimes this is not enough. On my visit I met with four elders (all women) and while their support for Forthspring was obviously strong, they were quite honest about continuing reservations among many church members. There was a process of consultation about changing the building's use, but in the end it was a close vote that decided the matter. David comments: 'At that time there were very few models to draw on. Through BBH's Value Sharing we have now met others pursuing the same path, and that is helping.'

One encouragement for the church has been the response of their senior citizens group to the changes. This group, which met before Forthspring came into being and has continued meeting in the newly refurbished building, has recently swelled the numbers at the weekly prayer group to unprecedented levels. Protestants and Catholics come, but the majority are Catholic. A weekly prayer group is common ground, I was told. 'Almost all are in the building anyway for their own activities, It is not like having to make a separate trip out on a Sunday', Sheila, one of the four elders, told me. 'It was the affirmation of this senior citizens group too that helped those of us at Forthspring through a real low recently', another said. I sensed the importance of this kind of affirmation. It was over ten years since I had last visited Belfast and at that time I was impressed by how hopeful many were about the future. There was such a groundswell then of people coming together because they wanted something different. In the wake of the peace process I might have expected some sense of achievement, but instead I met a kind of weary realism that seemed to be mostly about what had not happened. Certainly for me, driving through the Shankill and the Falls, little seemed to have changed. 'Indeed, things have become more entrenched. Both communities marking out their territory', Barbara, a volunteer at the Centre, told me. 'But of course we continue working for better relationships', David said. 'The alternative is too terrible to entertain.'

A bid to heal and develop relationships between the Catholic and Protestant communities is the focus of all the activities that take place at Forthspring. This means demonstrating practical means of reconciliation, encouraging non-violent alternatives to conflict, working to improve the quality of people's lives and reaching out to those most difficult to reach. At the heart of this is a community café. Coming into the café for a cup of tea or a simple meal is often the first step taken by a person apprehensive of venturing further, and there are plans to develop the café further. Forthspring has a full-time staff of eight and a team of international volunteers to run its projects. These include programmes for parents and toddlers, young people, women and senior citizens, a community relations programme and a counselling service. As a result of a recent evaluation the emphasis on proactive community relations work and prejudice awareness will be strengthened. Another outcome of the evaluation is a tricky one. Forthspring began as a partnership between mainly Christian bodies, with MISCA as a fourth partner. In fact, in the present climate it wouldn't have got off the ground at all, I was told, if Springfield Methodist Church, Cornerstone and The Currach had not taken the initiative. But now those who use the centre are wanting a greater community representation in its running.

The creation of Forthspring as a partnership has meant adjustment for its partners. MISCA no longer exists, but for Cornerstone and The Currach a period of adjustment and discernment has opened up new opportunities, including the chance to work with local churches. In doing this they are supporting the initiative of a Catholic Redemptorist priest,

Fr Gerry Reynolds, from the nearby Clonard Monastery. This initiative is simple but has proved amazingly effective, The idea is to have small teams of three or four Catholics visiting Protestant churches by agreement for their weekly services. They are there primarily to join in, but even when they do not speak their presence is always known and friendships have formed. As a result, last year's Nine Lessons and Carols at Clonard was attended by a number of Protestant churches. These and similar initiatives are now a focus for Cornerstone, while The Currach continues to build up work with women's and other 'issue' groups. Cornerstone and The Currach also provide a home for the many overseas volunteers that come to work at Forthspring

These four – Springfield Methodist Church, Cornerstone and The Currach and, out of their partnership, Forthspring Inter-Community Group – form a very strong 'net' along the Springfield Road. Each initiative has its own identity, but the partnership has enabled greater resources to be made available to the local community and – of equal importance certainly in their context – offers greater support for each partner. 'Such partnerships are, I think, the essential for the future', said David Campton. 'Not least it means we are not continually "reinventing the wheel", duplicating energy and resources. It enables good but maybe vulnerable ventures to continue and not go to the wall.'

My visit in mid-July meant that I missed the big march along the Springfield Road on the twelfth. It had been a particularly tense time again this year, but it had gone off better than many had feared; the uncertainty continues, however, about where the peace process is going now. Strangely, it was hard to leave. On the way out, Paul, a Protestant minister who earlier had given me a 'tour' of the city, stopped the car so that I could get out and write my name alongside the many others on the peace wall. Here positive and negative messages vie with each other. I wanted to leave something of myself behind, to add another positive symbol.

13

A neighbourhood centre in Scotland: Orbiston

I walked down the slipway from the railway station at Bellshill and stopped to get a feel for the area. To my right a row of shops, paint flaking and the betting shop and off-licence most prominent. To my left another betting shop and further down an amusement arcade and café. First impressions affirmed what I had already heard, that this was a rather 'grey' area. Not wholly grey; green spaces were interspersed with well-tended flower beds. These, together with the trim and orderly newish houses along the main road, gave another message, an attempt at least at regeneration of a run-down area. Yet there seemed to be a weariness in the air and in the faces of people I passed, young as well as old. Diminishment was the word that came to mind; life sapped by circumstances.

I had looked forward to coming to Bellshill and visiting the Orbiston Neighbourhood Centre (Orbiston is a post-war housing scheme located to the south of Bellshill). I had read the story several times of how the centre started. Perhaps now I was seeing what I expected to see, rather than the actual reality. I checked this out when I met Irene Gibson, the Projects Director at the centre. I told her how the word 'diminished' had come so clearly to mind. 'No, you're right', she told me. 'That's a fair description.' Money had come for new housing and flower beds, but Orbiston still has one of the highest unemployment figures for the whole of West Scotland. This is a situation that goes back to the closure of the nearby steel mills, which is also where the story I had read began.

In the light of what was happening to the area, the churches wanted to reach out and decided to do it through a children's mission. Local churches came together to work on the idea. A team came to help and Orbiston church was covered from top to bottom with silver foil. It was a magic castle. Many children came and loved it; they responded to the activities and to the message. Some parents came and joined in, but a few weeks later, when church members went to visit these and other families to invite them to come again, none were interested. It had been a one-off. That was all.

What to do next? Perhaps some other form of mission would work? An invitation came from the Urban Theology Unit in Sheffield, for one of the ministers to enrol in a course at UTU. Martin Johnstone, the Church of Scotland minister of St Andrew's and Orbiston Churches, was asked if he would like to go and agreed to do so. On his first visit he discovered that he was expected to have a small group back home who would be part of a process of action and reflection. He gathered such a group and their starting point was to listen to each other's life stories and experiences. It bonded them together very quickly; many of the stories reflected life as they experienced it in Bellshill at that time, stories of struggle and a lack of hope. Was this a reflection of others' lives, they wondered.

At this point they moved from listening to each other to listening to the community. All were engaged in going from house to house: How did those they visited feel about Bellshill as an area, what were some of its lacks, some of it good points, what needs did they have? They not only went from house to house but also interviewed the staff of local organizations and services. It was a daunting task for a small group, unused to doing this, but they grew in confidence throughout. What emerged was the need for a place where people could meet; there was no such place in Bellshill at that time. There were suggestions too as to how such a place could be used to meet the specific needs of the community.

Time now to act perhaps, but Martin and the group were involved in a process not only of action but reflection. They chose at this stage to take a step back and to spend a time reflecting on Scripture. What was the Spirit saying in this situation? They reflected on passages in Jeremiah and from St John's Gospel. What came to them was a new realization of how much the Bible has to say about God being with people in their struggles. With this came an assurance that God was with them in what they were doing, and they should now take some action. Could a place be found for such a centre?

A number of places were considered, but none were suitable or available. 'What about Orbiston Church? That would be suitable.' The question was put to Martin. This was a possibility he had not considered or bargained for and it brought about a deep personal struggle. 'I resolved the matter when I realized I either needed to go ahead or leave the ministry', said Martin. The whole experience had become one of personal conversion for him – to a new way of being church. The small group were already convinced of the way ahead. Now they began to consult and work with others in the community to raise funds and lay plans. The new centre was opened in August 1995.

Now six years later the centre was in front of me; the colourful, eye-catching signs welcoming me to 'a place for people, a centre for all'. The signage is new, paid for by Travel Inn. It is an important addition, as the centre is located in a side road and needs to make itself noticeable. All age groups are welcome, and those who come (over 1000 local people regularly each week) take part in a variety of activities. These include parents and toddlers, out of school care, youth work, computer training, a credit union, line dancing, yoga, weight watchers and day care for frail elderly people. These and other services are those identified as those most wanted by a survey of some 600 households.

There is also now an all-day café and a food cooperative. An increasing number come just to use the café; it is not necessary to enrol in other activities. The centre is first and foremost a 'meeting place where people from many different backgrounds and age groups can come together, learn from one another, and come to enjoy each others' company'. Behind this lies the 'desire to give practical expression to God's love for every person in the community'. That this desire lay behind the running of the centre was a fact that Eileen returned to several times in our conversation. It is its heart.

The centre incorporates the premises of Orbiston Parish Church in a novel way which ensures that church and centre keep cooperating. Eileen showed me a large hall with what I presumed was a stage at one end, curtained off. There was no stage as such; behind the red curtains lay the church's space, with the raised area for table and pulpit and chairs for Sunday worship piled in front. If a larger space is needed, as often happens, then the curtains are drawn back and the hall reverts to use as a church. That morning the hall was being used for carpet bowls by a number of 'frail elderly folk' assisted by young volunteers. I noticed that the cradle (baptismal) rolls still hang on the walls. It is shared space and that feels good, even if at times it brings frustration for both church and centre. Eileen had some good stories of having to juggle space on a number of occasions when circumstances demanded a quick negotiation, usually to accommodate funerals.

It takes a lot of people to run a centre like Orbiston. At the time I visited there were 21 people employed, many of whom live locally. Essential also are the volunteers, over 50 members of the local community. A number of these are church members, several of whom have been involved since the beginning of the centre and before. Their involvement is known and supported by the church congregation, but otherwise there seemed to be no real integration. Cooperation yes, but no more than that. There is disappointment among some church members that numbers at Sunday worship have not apparently grown since the centre opened. Eileen (who is a member of a parish church in Castlemilk) sees it a bit differently: 'You can see it as church happening here for a few one hour on Sunday, or as happening here seven days a week for many.' There is a daily service of worship in the centre, led by members of the churches in the town. 'It is one of the activities that we offer, no more or less important than any other.' Twice a week the daily service is well-attended by those coming for day care.

The small room was almost too small, a wheelchair and zimmer frame adding to the congestion. It was a good congestion and those who came were in good voice. That day the service was led by a Catholic nun from the nearby convent. A prayer, a reading, a short led reflection and several hymns or songs. These were well-known modern hymns, including 'Spirit of the Living God' and 'Bind Us Together, Lord', obviously well-known by those present and sung heartily. I commented on the singing to my neighbour and asked if she was a member of the church herself. 'No,' she told me, 'I'm a Catholic and so is Joan', indicating her friend. The centre is a place of ecumenism as well as a neighbourhood centre. From where I sat I could see through a window in the door immediately ahead to where the volunteers in the kitchen were moving around, stacking plates. A small corridor links the café and the meeting room, a deliberate arrangement to keep the spaces open and connecting. For me it added to the worship. The service over, we crammed into another corridor leading back into the main hall. Lively music met us and soon some were jigging back down to the main hall to the sound of 'Down by the Riverside'. Curious, I went to have a look, A small band – piano accordion and trumpet – were in full swing. The flow from one activity to the other again seemed very natural.

This six-year-old centre seemed to me to have huge potential for a growing and developing relationship with the church. This development, however, is at some risk. Martin moved on from being the minister in 2000; the appointment of his successor is key to this developing relationship. Martin was the minister of two churches in the town – St Andrew's and Orbiston parish churches. One suggestion has been for Orbiston to have its own minister, because the centre has opened up new opportunities for pastoral care that go beyond normal parish expectations. For Martin this happened naturally as he spent time in the centre. Financially, however, it seems unlikely that Orbiston will get its own minister. There has been some consultation between centre staff and church appointment bodies, but more as a second thought than a first. There is little confidence that the potential of the situation has been grasped or the centre's new model of church understood. This seems at odds with the fact that it is considered one of the 'most innovative and imaginative community based organizations currently operating', and one that has attracted widespread interest both locally and nationally. As well as participating in Building Bridges of Hope, it has been the subject of a number of TV programmes, including *Heart of the Matter*. If a creative and godly way forward is not found here, then it is likely that the centre will continue to operate with its founding ethos, but close links to the local church may be lost.

It costs a lot of money to build, run and develop a neighbourhood centre. One member of staff is employed full-time to raise funds. A number of different agencies and charities have funded development, including the Scottish Executive, Lanarkshire Development Agency, BBC's Children in Need and Lloyds TSB Foundation. 'Isn't it exhausting having to go continually cap in hand to funders?' I asked. Again, Eileen saw it differently: 'I see that it gives opportunity for others to put something back into the community. It is the way that is possible for them.' There are of course plans for the future. These include developing key aspects of the project as community businesses, run by local community members and employing local people. In this way the centre will be promoting economic as well as social environmental and spiritual improvement in the area.

A charitable company was set up in 1993 to develop the centre. It was given the name Utheo Ltd, short for Urban Theology Group. It is a reminder that all this began with a small group of people who came together to share stories, reflect on what they heard and act on what they heard God say. The group was disbanded a short while after the centre opened. This was felt to be in keeping with what was happening: not perpetuating the old, but entering into the new. A biblical theme leading up to the opening was that of the Abrahamic communities in the Old Testament who were also faced with the opportunities and dilemmas of leaving the familiar behind and embracing the unknown.

I left marvelling at how much had been achieved by the faith of just a few, and concerned that it should be given the time and resources to take the next steps as a new model of church.

14

Worship that connects: Glasgow's Late Late Service

I had expected to attend an alternative worship service in Glasgow on the Saturday evening, but it was postponed; most of the regulars were away on holiday. Instead I had lunch with Triona, Lesley and Chris and learnt about the Late Late Service that way.

An ecumenical Christian community is how the Late Late Service describes itself. It grew out of a Church of Scotland Youth Assembly in the 90s, when a group of young adults interested in alternative forms of worship were drafted in to help with the worship; it provided the catalyst for a new community initiative.

To begin with, the Late Late Service in Glasgow held its worship services in night clubs. Somehow the atmosphere was not right and after a while they began to use church venues instead. Most of those involved both then and now are young adults who had been around the church a while, but were feeling increasingly alienated by its worship style. Largely this had to do with language. 'Let's be honest,' said Chris, 'most of the language and imagery used in church services goes back to the age of the Enlightenment. It just doesn't communicate with our generation.' Nor, increasingly, with those older, I added. The search for new and relevant liturgy is no longer limited to the younger generation, we agreed.

As a Christian community, the Late Late Service is an 'expression of a like-minded group's relationship with God, and an attempt to make worship real, relevant, welcoming, participative and pleasing to God'. People come and go;

students move on, others move away. Numbers at the worship events fluctuate. The 'community base' is now quite small, only around a dozen; services are held perhaps only four times a year. I asked the three members I met whether the Late Late Service was also their church, or did they also belong to mainstream churches? For two at least this is their church. Their community life is built around time spent planning the services and as a group of friends they meet up quite naturally in the course of a week, not always in the same groupings. One of their beliefs is that church is not a place you visit on a Sunday morning but one which embodies who you are spiritually and actually.

The community, however, has very real links with the mainstream church. It is a member of ACTS (Action of Churches Together in Scotland) and locally has strong links with many denominations including the Church of Scotland, the Methodist Church and the Episcopal Church. At one time they moved their venues deliberately from church to church to cultivate these links, but practically it is easier for them to have one base. At present the local Church of Scotland church provides this base. The community is also asked to participate in local church events and they are happy to do this. There was, they said, no pressure put on them to become actual members; the local denominations are willing to let this Christian community have it own space and contribute its giftedness to the wider body.

The community's aim is broad:

- To have a democratic church where everyone has an equal opportunity to create and be involved in worship. This moves away from the traditional, patriarchal church where one individual, usually a man, stands at the front and the congregation listens.

- To have a Christian community which covers every aspect of our lives, for example sexuality, morality, happiness, grief, anger, pain.

- To actively work together to tackle social issues such as homelessness, abuse and environmental issues.

- To explore other faiths and traditions, such as Judaism and Buddhism, and learn what we can from them. Rather than 'watering down' our Christianity, the LLS believe this helps to create a more balanced, vibrant church.

- To keep seeking and creating new forms of prayer, meditation, liturgy and community that will be pleasing to God and accessible to society as a whole.

One change that has taken place is a move from celebrations to quieter worship events. I asked why this had happened. One reason, they felt, had to do with the stress experienced by many in society today. 'Or perhaps it's just that we are getting older.' Whatever the reason, this is now seen as one of the main ways forward. Such quiet services include led meditations and ways of incorporating the body in worship, things which help people to get in touch with their deeper selves, often dulled by the rush of life.

Exploring alternative forms of worship is at the heart of the Late Late Service's existence as a Christian community. Their aim is for their worship to be God-centric and culturally relevant and also in keeping with the common creeds of the Church. From the start, however, they found hymns too traditional and choruses culturally alienating. Many members had gifts in the theatre, film-making, the visual arts, writing and music, and so were able to create new worship music and expressions for their own services.

'But sometimes now I feel we are hardly radical', commented Triona. The other two nodded sympathetically. That is because many of the new worship forms have now been taken up by local churches and incorporated into mainstream services. This is not something they mind, but it may change the way the Late Late Service develops in the future. They have seen many changes already and flexibility is an important aspect of their lives 'Part of the "alternative" thing that we do is not to be afraid of changing how we do things.'

15

Clubbers in Edinburgh

'You should also visit the Club Church in Edinburgh', Martin Johnstone told me, so I went there following my lunch with the Late Late Service. I had misunderstood what had been said when I phoned to make the arrangement. I was expecting to take part in a worship event. When I rang to tell Fiona my train was late and I was delayed, she said (I thought), 'There are quite a few of us. Slip in the back.' Immediately a hall and rows of chairs came to mind, a stereotype. What she had said was, 'There are quite a few of us. We'll be in the back.' At the back of the coffee bar, I was to discover!

It took a while for me to reorientate myself. The 'few of us' were a group of twelve or so men and women – T-shirted, fit and sun-tanned – absorbed in vigorous debate. The pile of glasses, cups and plates piled on the table said that this had been going on for some while. Conversation flowed around me; those nearest pulled their chairs closer and answered my questions. The Club meets every Sunday afternoon from 1 till 3. Club is not actually the word they use, but it has been used of them. What was happening here was much more informal than that. Well, not too informal: three of those present were part-time project workers – a team of 'enablers', helping to make things happen.

The initiative had come from St Cuthbert's, a Church of Scotland congregation in the West End of Edinburgh's city centre. St Cuthbert's is a historic building that has seen many changes during its long history; more recent changes have redefined who its parishioners are. A survey showed that while 2000 lived in the area, 8000 worked there, and at weekends another 20,000 came, drawn by the range of entertainment on offer. What was needed, the church concluded, was a variety of different spaces where people of different interests could meet and find a place to explore matters of concern and faith in depth, without any strings attached. An initiative was started with those at work, and this was followed by contacting those in the club scene to see if a similar project would be welcomed.

Clubs were visited, video interviews conducted with clubbers, magazines and literature consulted, talks initiated with community education and youth workers involved in sexual health and drugs awareness. The thought had been to appoint a pastoral advisor – a chaplain – to work in a local night club, but research changed this direction. It was decided instead to facilitate the establishment of a small core Christian community in and for club culture, and to start with the part-time team of three. Those who formed this community would be actively involved, seen and known as part of the local club scene and translators of Christianity within it. Behind this was the desire to make a reconnection between the tradition of the historic church and present culture and to create a space or spaces where this might happen.

The gathering in the bar that Sunday afternoon was just such a space. This was an informal, easy conversation space. Other spaces have been created, one a worship space. I wondered who felt drawn. Clubbers with an interest in spirituality, who wanted something more than the club scene itself offered, I was told. Also young adults dissatisfied with what mainstream churches offered them. I wanted to know more about the worship space and what happened there. Paul, one of the team, told me that it is highly participatory. An aim is to get everyone involved, not for any one person to lead. He gave as an example a worship time when 'stations' had been set up around the church. Each station represented a 'beatitude' and different groups took responsibility for how each was developed. Another example was of a communion service where its various parts were given out to those who came, who then took responsibility for those parts. 'It is not that we are trying to change anything as such, but seeking ways to worship that come from our own lives and experience.' At the start such worship times took place in the clubs themselves, but this has changed back to church venues as more practical and easier to find than some of the clubs! This is similar to the Late Late Service's experience.

Is the Edinburgh Club Church a new form of church? Any kind of definition is considered warily: 'The way we would explain what happens here to those in the club scene is very different to the way we try to explain it to church members.' Dissatisfaction with the mainstream churches is not a carping dissatisfaction. Being supported by and having links to the traditional Church is considered essential. But there is an inherent challenge to traditional forms. 'Traditionally the churches have their services around 10.30 on a Sunday. That cuts out most of the population, who are just getting up at that time. Most come alive at night-time – certainly in the scene we relate to.'

16

Laying ghosts in Teesside

'I've been changed just by living here', Imelda commented.

We were sitting in the car waiting to be transported in midair across the Middlesbrough Transporter Bridge, the only remaining working bridge of its kind in Europe. The ferry is held on massive pulleys and moves in the air, not on the water – a moving platform. There was time left before my departure to experience this new-to-me form of transportation. Much of the day had also been taken up with talk of a new way, new models, a new approach – again to church.

'What do you mean by changed?' I asked Imelda, a Catholic Sister.

'You know that film where the teacher asks the pupils to get up and all stand on their desks. He asked them to do that to help them see things from a different perspective. It's been like that for me, seeing life from a different perspective – the way people living here see and experience life. We're often cushioned in life from the starkness of what life is like for those who have nothing or very little. Once you see things from a totally different perspective, that perspective colours everything. It changes you.'

In a small way I had experienced that 'difference' while travelling by train to Teesside. Alighting from the Flying Scotsman that had brought me to Darlington from Glasgow – comfortable seating, adequate leg room, minimal number of passengers – I was within minutes aboard a crowded two-carriage train that lurched out of the station. I stumbled and found myself looking into the steely gaze of a woman I had fallen against; unnerving, had there not been also a steadying hand and a glint of a smile. It was summer and children crawled about, squabbled, cried and added to the general mayhem. On that journey and on the way back the small train was totally inadequate for the number of users, and on the return journey it broke down altogether. Not long out of the station the landscape began to change. Vast cooling towers, sand blasters and other strange steel edifices crowded the landscape, like something out of science fiction. At Middlesbrough I had to fight my way to the door to get off. The contrast to the rest of the journey was stark, a culture shock.

'This is the largest area of chemical industry in the whole of Europe', Imelda informed me. Much of the infrastructure is, however, a relic of a past age. The iron, steel and shipbuilding industries of the last two centuries have now been largely replaced by chemical industries. Not that these new industries have benefited local people much; pollution has increased rather than decreased, new firms rely more on computers than people, contract work has replaced jobs for life.

I was making my way to Port Clarence, which a newspaper report in 1988 – just before Imelda and her colleague Philippa came to the area – called a 'ghost town'. Rumour had it that the town was going to be demolished. It was only a rumour but general mistrust was such that some believed it. 'Nuns hit ghost town' was the headline in this local paper that same year. This was not a headline that the local people or Imelda and Philippa would have wanted, but the article was good and helped to introduce the Sisters to the local people. 'We didn't have to work so hard to introduce ourselves.'

Imelda Poole and Philippa Green are IBVM (Loreto) Sisters (Philippa was away the day I visited). Their congregation was founded 400 years ago by Mary Ward, a Yorkshirewoman who was called to found an international apostolic order for women. Until a few years ago Imelda worked as a youth employment training officer; Philippa was an educational psychologist. Both had become frustrated at the inability of the statutory services to understand and meet the real needs of people. In the 1980s the Order met for a general congregation to reflect on its mission and future; one outcome was a commitment to a 'a preferential order for the poor'. One result was that Imelda and Philippa were sent by the congregation to find a place where this call could be lived out. Four areas were suggested to them – one in Wales, one in Ireland and two in England. They chose the North East and the Clarences (the collective name for Port and High Clarence), a community of around 450 households – an 'urban island' in the midst of a sea of chemical firms. On one of their first visits they wandered into the community centre and were struck by the welcome they received as visitors. They were not identifible as nuns at the time, but it was as if they had found their home.

Another factor in choosing Port Clarence was the fact that there was no church building at all in the area. There had been five, but they had all been demolished. Some lived gospel presence in the area was called for. The local council was approached about housing to rent. It was now known that Imelda and Philippa were Sisters and their reasons for wanting to come. The Residents Association was consulted and 'it was the association that chose our home for us'. A small but adequate three-bedroomed terrace house with a small garden back and front. By this time local churches in the wider area had also been consulted about the Sisters' arrival; all were supportive. The Catholic Church had continued to have a presence in the Clarences, using homes or, latterly, the community centre as a mass centre. Other ministers – URC, Anglican and Methodist – had also led services from time to time at the community centre; the URC minister was well-known for his pastoral care and support of families in the area.

When Imelda and Philippa moved in, the house was still in a half-finished state, with boards up at the door and windows. Repairs had had to be done to make it habitable.

When they arrived they discovered that there had already been an attempt to break in: the lock had been damaged. Again, however, a negative situation turned into a positive, as one by one concerned neighbours arrived to help. So many people came and went that getting settled took far longer than expected. Still, it was a heartening start.

That was thirteen years ago. 'Social entrepreneurs' is how one local body, the NESEF, describes much of what they are about. A reporter wrote in the NESEF magazine:

> Imelda and Philippa do not have a specific project, but see their role as listening to the people about their concerns and helping them take action to address certain issues. They self-reference not as social entrepreneurs but more as workers for social justice helping the local people themselves to take action and find solutions.

Soon after their arrival in the Clarences a neighbour arrived with a list of people she thought Imelda and Philippa might visit. They were the names of people who had felt particularly abandoned when the last of the churches was knocked down. Imelda and Philippa were glad to follow this up, but did so by beginning to visit all the houses on the estate. Again there was a ready welcome, people glad to see them and eager to talk. Sometimes on a practical level they were able to help, more often than not it was just a matter of being there to listen. Often the matters raised highlighted situations of injustice that needed to be addressed. One that surfaced early on had to do with health.

The climate in this part of the North East is particularly damp and raw and itself affects health. Add to this pollution from the chemical industry, and the situation becomes acute. For many, stress and bad diet exacerbate the problems. Until recently, however, health provision on the estate was either poor or non-existent. Latterly, the nearest health centre was in Billingham, four miles and a bus ride away, which discouraged many from making the journey at all. There had been an attempt by local residents to campaign for a change but this had not got far, due to tiredness and lack of skills. The more recent campaign has been successful: five years of often frustrated lobbying has resulted in medical provision being available at the newly opened Community and Enterprise Centre. I visited the centre with Imelda just days after it had been opened. A bright, newly painted, functional building with a full-time nurse practitioner and medical receptionist and with doctors and other professionals attending on a part-time basis. 'It will take a while before people start coming. They are so unused to the provision being here. But they will come', I was told. The first few days had been encouraging.

It had taken a lot of work by local people to get the Health Centre. Information had to be gathered (a community health survey), public meetings held and a lot of local council members and other bodies lobbied. Imelda and Philippa discovered that officials of public bodies like to stay on their own ground with a modus operandi in which they present the issues and explain the actions they are taking to tackle them. More effective is encouraging local people to engage in a dialogue instead of receiving a presentation. That moves the goalposts and new possibilities open up.

Another issue was related to the fact that there was no pay point on the estate. Fuel poverty is the name given by local people to the lack of a pay point which would enable them to pay gas and electricity bills in cash and avoid the use of expensive pre-payment meters. This was one of the issues where justice was at stake. Those who can pay bills by direct debit are automatically granted a discount which those on lower incomes are denied. Pay points do something to rectify this injustice; however, it has to be in close proximity to local customers, not some four miles and a £3 return bus fare away. When the matter was raised with the local council, they said installation of a pay point at Port Clarence was not viable because too few people would use it. Teesside Church Action on Poverty, which meets in Imelda and Philippa's house every month, took up the matter and worked with local residents to conduct a door to door survey showing not only that unemployment on the estate was 80 per cent, but that 75 per cent of residents would use a local pay point. A public meeting was held and within two months the campaign had achieved its goal. This campaign, like the campaign to improve health provision and other such campaigns (such as tackling the problem of rats on the estate and of flooding due to an unattended blocked culvert in a river) has brought local people together in a new way. A strong network has emerged of individuals and organizations both secular and religious – another 'network of goodwill'. 'A sign of God's kingdom', Imelda would say.

Imelda and Philippa came to Port Clarence to be a church presence in the midst of a council estate, where four church buildings had been demolished over twenty years before. Their focus for ministry is that of befriending; 'pre-evangelization ministry if you like'. They soon discovered that there were many people on the estate who had a real sense of God and a connection to church that was deeply rooted and went back generations. For many people the fact that all the churches in the the Clarences had been demolished had served to heighten their sense of deprivation, of being a forgotten place. The church buildings had been places where the community gathered not only for funerals and weddings but for other occasions too. That most people did not or could not attend a place of worship did not mean that they were indifferent. When the last Roman Catholic church was demolished, 'the community lost its centre', a resident told Imelda and Philippa. It is this background that they feel has been behind the welcome they have received from an estate which had a very strong sense of community but has suffered from years of neglect. Now respect is returning – a sense of personal self-worth and pride in their surroundings.

Since the coming of the Sisters, and in response to people's needs, regular ecumenical worship of different kinds has taken place. In the past much of this worship took place in the local community centre, but since the closure of the centre by the local council, who were unable to pay for its upkeep, the worship has mostly taken place in Imelda and Philippa's house – or out on the streets. The latter is for more seasonal acts of worship, but not when the weather is too cold. There is also no quiet place on the estate for people to go to when they are grieving, stressed or in need of a bit of breathing space: a place just to *be*. Imelda spoke of people 'sometimes needing a quiet place to cry'. I thought of a similar comment made by Eileen at Kingston Terrace in Leeds.

An actual place of worship – a building – is therefore important. When the community centre was shut overnight, there was suddenly nowhere for people to gather. That Sunday all that remained of the church's belongings was carried up the street to the nearby Enterprise Centre, which had been suggested by the locals as a makeshift church. One of the residents, not a churchgoer, came to Philippa and Imelda and said that church worship needed to carry on in the community, so why not use this place until something was sorted. Then the Enterprise Centre was closed too, but only for refurbishment. It has now been reopened as the Clarences Community and Enterprise Centre.

The new centre includes an innovative new medical provision, a food cooperative, youth and crèche provision and a welcoming reception area. This has all come about through local people finding they can have a voice and are able to work together to achieve what they need for their own community. There is something more. It is hoped that funds can now be raised to roof the courtyard that links the various units of the new centre; this will provide the large gathering space which the community so badly needs. It is also hoped that a Peace Centre will be established as one unit of this new complex. The courtyard itself can also be used for larger acts of worship. It is a wonderfully creative concept, embracing all aspects of local life and putting celebration, reflection and worship at the heart of it.

That this new feature should be called a Peace Centre rather than a church is the result of a lot of reflection. It is essential that whatever new church initiative happens is ecumenical. From the start Imelda and Philippa had and continue to have the full support of local churches of all denominations. What has been happening, has happened ecumenically. What has happened is also new – a new way of being community, a new way of expressing faith, a new model of church. The concept of the Peace Centre captures all this, it is a way of embracing the future. The area at the back of the Clarences is a large wasteland which attracts a wide variety of birds and other wildlife and whose wetlands are a home for seals; this will become an international nature reserve. A lot is happening on Teesside. A Peace Centre in the Clarences seems more than appropriate.

17

From pub to church: The Furnival in Sheffield

A huddle of people around a wooden table; a woman with a baby in a pram; some young people; a woman in a wheelchair. All just passing the time, it seemed. Behind them is a somewhat unimaginative square building; not much like a pub, but I recognized it from the large words THE FURNIVAL painted boldly across its front. Still, The Furnival is no longer a pub; I was told later that some locals now proudly proclaim that it is 'a church', though one with a difference. In 1996, when it became known that Lopham Street Chapel was wanting to buy the pub, there was local opposition: they preferred to keep their pub. That solution, however, was not on the cards and today it is recognized that The Furnival as it is now has brought new life to the area.

The story of The Furnival as a church cannot be separated from the story of the area. Pye Bank/Woodside is on the north east of the city, an area of extreme deprivation that literally overlooks a valley of grand buildings, affluence and bustling commerce. Sheffield is a city, I was told, where the extremes of poverty and affluence are sharper than almost anywhere else in the country. Pye Bank/Woodside was not always on the poverty side; the running down of the steel industry in the 70s was its ruin, a general exodus from the area a result.

The chapel was also affected by the exodus: a once lively and growing congregation reduced to a just a handful. The chapel itself was closed and the site sold to a housing association in 1995. For the few members that remained there was only one way to maintain a worshipping core: they began to meet in each other's homes. They believed that the church still had a future in Pye Bank/Woodside, a contribution to make. One member, in her eighties, was certain of it. 'We just knew we had to stay, and that God was planning something new', she said later.

During this period there were plans for a new multipurpose church building but they never seemed to get anywhere. In 1996 it became known that one of the few pubs in the area was going to be put up for sale. The small congregation saw its opportunity and decided to buy it if they could; it was sold to them at auction for just under £50,000. On Palm Sunday 1996 a symbolic walk became an act of worship – a walk from Lopham Street to The Furnival in Verdon Steet in the very heart of the estate. There has been no attempt to change its 'pubbish' look (its very familiarity is an asset), nor to make it into just a worship centre. The changes that have been made to the building have been done to accommodate the needs of the local community.

'I came one day and stood just across the street.' Peter indicated the spot he meant. 'I sat there a long time and just looked. I knew then that this was the place I had to be, that I didn't want to be anywhere else.' Peter had intended training for the priesthood, indeed had begun to do so. At the time he was at seminary and had come to the area on a placement with the local Catholic church. That moment of illumination just outside Verdon Street Post Office changed all that. He had begun to find seminary training stifling and too academic; what he wanted was to be engaged with the surrounding reality. He has certainly found that at The Furnival, where he has now worked for the past five years, sometimes on a paid basis, sometimes voluntarily. Currently he is chair of the Executive Committee. 'I think this is the best possible training for the priesthood, although whether that's now where I'm headed I'm not sure', he said. For the moment Peter is still where he wants to be.

A similar sense of calling to The Furnival was experienced by others. Early on, a Baptist minister came, then a young man with gifts in music, followed by two Roman Catholic Sisters and then a young woman – all with a sense of being called to the area; others were to follow. From the start the new beginnings at The Furnival were ecumenical, for those of different denominations and none. A number who came took up residence in the terraced flats adjoining the pub's courtyard. Indeed, nearly all those involved live in the area, the majority settled over many years, and many of them still have a strong sense of being rooted there, of not wanting to leave despite the disadvantages.

The wider area of Burngreave, of which Pye Bank/Woodside is a ward, is densely multi-cultural, 'perhaps one of the most multi-cultural areas in the country'. 'People here, however, live peaceably together; there are no race riots. There are no ghettos', Peter told me. 'Ethnically, the different groups have been settled here a long time. Areas are mixed there are many mixed marriages; second generation marriages too.' A large multi-cultural festival had been held the week before with no trouble. The big problem for the local area is drugs; this is a periodic rather than a continuing problem. 'When the police do a sweep in or near the town centre, then the problem moves over here.' When that happens, The Furnival is aware of it. The natural gathering point just outside the pub is also a convenient spot for passing on drugs. This has raised questions about the advisability of allowing people to gather there. Removing the table and chairs and discouraging gathering and conversation also has its obvious downside. There are rarely easy answers.

The pub's frontage is at least open and lit. Previously, the paved area to one side of the pub drew a lot of unwanted activity and was dark and full of debris. This has changed; the area has become an attractive courtyard with raised flower-beds and a few young trees growing. More colour is provided by the hanging baskets outside individual flats and the dense splashes of colour in the small gardens of the ground-floor flats below; the Baptist minister Jane's garden is easy to identify by its sprawling vine and the profusion of flowers in a small space. 'And the litter bin', Peter pointed out. The bin was the first bit of neighbourhood regeneration to be put in place; like the hanging baskets it was provided by the council. The new residents have helped to bring a new feel to this part of Verdon Street. Jane Grinnoneau, the Baptist minister, is a keen gardener; she is also Minister and Projects Coordinator at the centre.

Changes like this come about through working in partnership with many others: partnership with Sheffield City Council and local organizations concerned with youth, education, mental health and concern for the aged; partnership with housing associations and local trusts; partnership with local churches – Baptist, Methodist, United Reformed and with Churches Together in South Yorkshire; partnership most particularly with local people. These are real working partnerships, where relationships of respect and trust are built up and areas of common concern are faced head-on together. I picked up from Peter his very real concern that I should understand the importance of such relationships here, that they are the bedrock for all that has and can happen. The networking is a part of creating a new way of being church together, common values acting as building blocks.

One foundational relationship is with the locally based Urban Theology Unit. Opened in 1973 as a centre for the discovery of Christian mission and vocation, UTU has supported and enabled many such initiatives, locally and further afield. The support here is mutual: students are often sent to The Furnival on placement. 'Not all', Christine Jones Director of Studies, told me. 'Some are too nervous to venture into Pye Bank/ Woodside.' For Christine herself and other staff at UTU The Furnival offers an essential balance to academia.

Peter and I had come out onto the courtyard to see some recent developments. Three shops adjacent to The Furnival became vacant in 1999. The Furnival acquired all three and launched Verdon Street Enterprises. One of the shops now sells secondhand clothes, another is a help centre and a third is rented to a Healthy Housing Initiative. Here being in touch and in partnership with Sheffield City Council is essential. Even more important is being in touch with and responding to local needs. In September 1999 a public consultation event was held. The result was a six-page document, the 'wish list' of local people. Some wishes were small and easily met – a permanent ideas box, citizens' advice for bills and small legal matters, TV with teletext facilities. Others were much larger – a mini gym, a health advice clinic, a cultural centre and music school. From the start listening to 'local people who tell us what they need' has been paramount. It is on this point that Furnival members are critical of the government's 'new deal for communities' for its frequent failure to take seriously the voices of local people, particularly those 'at the edge'. The need, therefore, for intermediary bodies that can both listen to and enable local action, is paramount. The Furnival is such an intermediary.

While Peter was talking to a passer-by I wandered off. An alleyway to the side of the courtyard led to a breathtaking view of the city centre in the distance and also to the sight of a large derelict building or block; its windows were boarded up but otherwise it seemed habitable. As Peter joined me I joked, 'Here's somewhere else for you to develop!' 'We hope so!' he told me in all seriousness. I was continually surprised throughout my visit by the extent of what had already been achieved at The Furnival and what is hoped for next. A bid has been made for this building – at present a block of 66 one-bedroom flats called Neville Drive – and plans put forward for development. A number of things from the local 'wish list' can be met if this goes ahead: working units for neighbourhood family learning, a healthy living centre, enterprise workshops, and childcare facilities, freeing parents for locally based learning. Everything depends on successful funding applications. If funding goes ahead Neville Drive will act as a bridge between the area and employment opportunities down in the valley. From our vantage point Peter pointed out the sweep of new development in the nearby Don Valley and city centre.

Within our view, he told me, lay a third of all jobs in the city. But here again intermediate steps are needed to enable local people to be able to access such jobs – a bridge.

In our walkabout Peter and I were now on the other side of The Furnival. I saw the launderette that had opened in response to local requests. There are two regular washing machines operated by coin slots and one heavy duty machine which will take duvets and other heavier items. There was also an iron and ironing board available. No one was in charge, access was throughout the day and on trust and there has been no vandalism, no scrawling on the walls. Underneath the launderette was the old pub cellar, now converted into an informal place for young people excluded from school. The programme is coordinated by Una Burke, one of the two Sisters who moved to the area in 1996. The cellar is now wonderfully equipped to respond to the needs of 11–16-year-olds who are not able to engage with school in the normal way. The demand for places from local comprehensives has grown rather alarmingly since the project was started. The Joseph Rank Benevolent Trust is a major funder.

Feeling rather overwhelmed, I went back again to the place that is quite definitely at the heart of The Furnival – the café. Here a pub bar has been turned into a community café; simple, inviting, busy. There is a play area for children and a variety of leaflets giving local information are pinned around the walls. From these I learnt that it is possible to access the local credit union here once a week, and on a Friday get advice and information on available jobs from Job Link. All this happens in the café, which is open from 10 till 3, Tuesday to Friday, and can also be hired for small events. Anyone can drop in whether or not they use the rest of the centre. While I was there a number did just this, drifting in for a drink or a bag of crisps. Josie, who manages the café, used to be one of those who drifted in in this way. Her story says a lot about the way The Furnival as a Christian community is touching lives.

Josie was one of those who thought The Furnival's new owners 'a joke really'. She was also curious about what really went on at times inside. She persuaded her daughter to come with her to a Sunday service. 'I'm just here for a bit of a laugh', she said. She came a second time 'again for a bit of laugh', but the third time she knew something had got to her. It was Jane Grinnoneau's turn to be surprised when Josie asked to be baptized. 'I knew I was loved. That's what made the difference', Josie said. Josie's new sense of her self-worth is enabling her to think differently about her life and faith. She was someone who had never had a job, apart from a spell working as an inmate in a prison kitchen. Now she is the Catering Manager, in charge of The Furnival's café. Previous to that she had been a Trainee Manager and the day I was visiting she received her Certificate of Achievement NVQ Level 2. It was a proud moment and she obviously loved every moment of it.

At the heart of The Furnival is a faith community made up of Christians from different denominations or none. Their mission statement is simple: 'to make real in the experience of the neighbourhood, the living presence of God'. Members of the congregation make up a council which oversees the life of The Furnival (property, faith community, etc.). Responsibility for oversight of all the project work is delegated to an executive committee. Services are held each Sunday, at the moment for children in the morning and for adults in the afternoon. Some services are led by the Furnival Team, others by local ministers. There is art, dialogue and group sharing, particularly when the Furnival Team are responsible, but Peter admitted that the congregation likes something more traditional most of the time. The meeting room where the services are held is another of the pub's two bars, and indeed both the original seating and the bar itself have been kept. The room still has the feel of a pub about it, more so than the café, 'We wanted to keep it like that', Peter told me. The congregation of around twenty to thirty is quite eclectic. As well as local people (that includes most of the Furnival Team) there are the many visitors who come from other parts of the city, drawn by the warmth and breadth. I wondered if there were attempts to reach out liturgically to the wider community. At Christmas time all the local churches visit and sing carols, but not to raise money; indeed, just the opposite: mince pies come free with the carols. 'A bit trad', said Peter. On the other hand he told me about the response to the anniversary of the Hillsborough Disaster: a service held then was advertised locally and many came to it. Peter felt it was important to be sensitive to such opportunities, but it is more important just to be there in the community and to do so openly as church.

This kind of openness happens every working day at The Furnival. At 8.45 am the staff meet in the café before it opens, a candle is lit and there is a short time of sharing and prayer. Once a week it is longer and includes a business meeting. The candle is lit for this too and the meeting ends with prayer. This meeting happened the day I was there, with Jane Grinnoneau in the chair. The sharing was about staff training, contracts, holidays, outings, funding applications; Josie was congratu-lated on receiving her Certificate of Achievement. There was need now for a new catering assistant; the job had been advertised but not yet filled. One of the café volunteers was asked if she was interested in the job. 'I could be,' she said, 'but I don't live here. I think it should be a local person.' Everyone nodded. The policy is to employ local people, in particular to provide training. By the end of the meeting people were beginning to crowd into the café; the door had been open throughout. We had not yet prayed, and when we did so, everyone in the café was quiet. I could see what Peter meant about doing things openly.

Throughout my visit, two words or phrases came up constantly – 'relational' was one and 'wrap around care' another. The Furnival is about building relationships – between themselves as a faith community, with local people, with government and other agencies, and with wider

Christian networks, BBH being one. 'That is the only way it works', Peter told me. Wrap around care is taking that one step further – 'staying with people daring to move from the edge, for as long as it takes – in order that new opportunities can be accessed'.

There was more but too much to absorb in one day. It was all very impressive but I knew that The Furnival, like other initiatives of its kind, is always vulnerable, not least because it is dependent on outside funding and often on the enthusiasm and gifts of particular individuals. 'But if we are not here tomorrow, we have done something today. Others can build on it', came the comment.

As I left, a completely different group of 'locals' had gathered around the table outside. That space around the table had become kind of symbolic for me – of church in the heart of the community.

18

Reflections: Ways forward

A prayer group, a theology group, the boldness of two women, the faithfulness of four, all of this is what lies behind these initiatives. The simplicity of it is breathtaking; the implications huge. Two years ago I edited a booklet for New Way, entitled *Small and in Place: Practical Steps in Forming Small Christian Communities*. It contained nine stories of such initiatives, three of the places are included in this book. Kathy Galloway, theologian, poet and community activist, wrote a reflection. She wrote of these 'shoots of new life':

> In-between times are times of re-evaluation, and often those taking the lead in this are on the margins of the church. I believe it is the work of the Holy Spirit that there are so many struggling local churches, so many small groups, so many little loving, faltering communities who have embraced the deaths required of them to sow seeds of resurrection for the rest of us. They remind me of another faltering little community which departed from the old pattern to follow the living patterns of Jesus the Word made flesh.

These living patterns, she wrote, are characterized by movement, by being very close to the lives of a community, by profound questioning, by corporateness, by visibility, by the importance of the role played by women and lay people, and by singular and intense personal attachment to Jesus.

Implicit in these comments by Kathy Galloway is both the fragility of many of these ventures, and the call to the rest of us to learn from them; we too are called to death and resurrection. What the stories do are point some ways forward; four come to mind.

Giving significance or meaning to people's experiences

Twice now, small ad hoc liturgy groups in the place where I live have enabled ecumenical community celebrations to take place in the parish church. On both occasions we wanted to find a way to celebrate life in our community. At the first we invited local businesses and organizations to come and place symbols by the communion table as a mark of their place in the community. The local school rang to ask if they could erect display boards in the chancel; they wanted to mark the work and departure of those leaving school that year. The school band played in the service, its jazz band at the celebration afterwards. The second celebration came not long after an arson attack on the school; its main hall and science block had been completely destroyed together with much sixth form practical exam work. That it happened at all was a shock to the whole village. For this service a group of students wrote a ballad – a history of Lytchett Minster – ending with lines about the fire, and the celebration offered an occasion for corporate recognition of grief.

Many of those who came to these services had not been into a church for a considerable time. These in particular came up afterwards to say how important a happening it had been for them; something significant had happened, a meaning had been given. I do not see this as a step to getting people to come to church on a more regular basis (although this may happen), but as finding a multiplicity of ways to enable church to happen where people are.

Offering a variety of different spaces

The minister of St Cuthbert's Church in Edinburgh had in mind the concept of 'creating spaces' where people can find wholeness, promote respect for the earth and experience social justice. In particular he followed this through in relation to the business community and the club scene. This idea of 'creating spaces' seems to me to be important. Again, where I live a number of such spaces have emerged in the last two to three years. From the initiative of one or more individuals, groups have formed around an interest in theology, spirituality, women's issues, global injustice; there is also a prayer group that meets monthly and explores creativity and meditative prayer. Most of the people who come to these groups do not attend any regular place of worship, although most have at some point in the past. All these groups are connected in some way or another with more mainstream churches; they are not breakaway groups, nor do they desire to be.

Giving space to

In offering a variety of 'church spaces' that reach out to people in their interests and concerns, it seems essential, on the evidence of these stories, that there is no coercion, no proselytizing. The concept of giving space to or taking space is what movement is all about, space for individuals and for groups to explore faith in a new way.

I first came across this concept of 'being given a space' when I visited European basic Christian communities in the 1980s. Basic communities have existed for the most part on the edges of the mainstream Church in Europe – a different experience from those in other parts of the world. Their desire has been for 'relationship and dialogue with the institutional church so that we may share our insights on the one church as we journey. Our goal is to have some possibility to change church and society.' A member of an Italian community commented: 'What we are struggling for is a change in the institution so that it makes room to allow our experience to have its impact.'

Learning from

To visit over a period of three months so many brave and challenging ventures – bridges of hope – is to be changed in the process. The visits coming so close together might have made me think that places like this are the norm across the country, but of course they are not. Reading about them may not be the same as spending time alongside them. Eileen Carroll wrote in her report to her congregation, 'Come and see'. There is something very important here. What I have been writing about is not another programme for church renewal; it is about a mind shift, a matter of the heart, a conversion. Nearly all those I have talked to have at some point experienced a shock of the heart, a conversion. This – as Jonathan Cotton would say – is about love in all its stark simplicity: about love of people, where they are at and who they are. It is important to experience this for ourselves.

I have mentioned several times in this reflection the fragility of these ventures. The fragility is real; what balances it are the many partnerships and networks that are spawned by the inherent movement. There is a sense in which the networking itself becomes a new way of being church. This networking – of churches, between groups and agencies and in partnership with secular organizations – is in many places building new communities – local communities and communities of interest – that speak powerfully of God's reign, of the kingdom, or kin-dom.

We are not just talking here of what is small!

Other journeys

19

A parish in good heart in Plymouth

It was not possible to include St Barnabas, Stoke, Plymouth (St B's) in the 'three journeys', but I have made many journeys there in recent years. One was in January 2000 to facilitate a parish weekend, together with Michael Bridgwater, also from New Way. We had been 'accompanying' the parish for the previous two years, making regular visits to listen and encourage. Ron Ram was also visiting St B's that same weekend. Afterwards I wrote a 'memory' of the visit which I include here. An update on developments at St B's since then follows this 'memory'.

January 2000

It seems that in the last year a profound change has taken place at St B's. A church already on the way has gained a new sense of direction. The members recognize this, John Summers, the vicar, recognizes it, and Ron, who has been visiting the church over the past three years as a participant observer, sees it even more clearly. 'On the ground you don't always recognize such change', admits John. It seem that this growth has come about mostly as a result of John's absence, a fact that make us all chuckle, John included. A three month's sabbatical and taking on responsibility for another nearby church mean that John is often absent. Now, after a number of years learning about a ' new way', the penny has dropped; the small congregation has owned the fact that 'they are the church'.

We are meeting in a small room with inadequate heating and only the bravest take their coats off. It is, however, warmer here than in the rest of this barn of a church, which is being sold ('soon we hope'). Margaret, Ruth, Jane, Lisa and David are a few of those present, who number altogether a dozen or so, some in caring or other professions, the majority elderly retired folk. 'We're a pretty ordinary bunch.' Not perhaps a very likely lot to carry forward a new vision, but they are proving otherwise.

These lay members, together with others, run the church. John is there but he takes a back seat. The people are the church and it is their church. The focus is the neighbourhood and in each geographical area there is a 'neighbourhood group' – what John calls the 'local basic unit of church'. Those who make up these groups are all active in the community in different ways, and see contributing to its welfare as an integral part of mission. Here in Stoke this has meant supporting the Residents' Association and the credit union, enabling groups for mothers and toddlers and over 50s to start and, more recently, responding to the request to help start a youth club. The emphasis on enabling and supporting, not 'doing things' for the community, is paying off. Indeed, so few members could not otherwise sustain the many commitments.

In many ways all this is not so different from some other churches. Most churches run activities for local people. But these 'local units' or 'neighbourhood groups' are more integrated into the community, more known. One group was approached by the local health clinic and asked if they would run a candlelit service for the clinic in the run up to Christmas. This event is still talked about; it made its mark on both the local community and on the members of St B's; it was an affirmation that they are doing 'something right'!

There is a parish church to run as well and members of neighbourhood groups serve on the parochial church council and on various committees (the future of 'the barn of a building' takes up a lot of time). Once a month a neighbourhood group is responsible for the Sunday liturgy. On other Sundays individual lay members plan and lead the service, supported by local clergy if it is a communion service. Sometimes that is John!

'One need that I see is to build up a more reflective awareness of what's going on', John said to Mike and myself. We took this up with those who came to the weekend and suggested that we reflect on one part of the life of the church. They chose to reflect on the Tuesday Tea Break, a club for the over 50s. Mike and I suggested a process that would be something like peeling away the layers of an onion. 'That can make you cry!' someone astutely commented. This is what followed.

Telling the story

Members divided into two groups, each group preparing a five-minute presentation of the Tea Break story, using non-verbal means as far as possible. One chose a local radio interview; the other a more visual presentation, 'for TV maybe'. The story that emerged went something like this.

> We held a survey to find out what the local community wanted. We followed this up with a public meeting in church. What was most needed was a place for the over 50s, particularly those who live on their own. As a result we started the Tuesday Tea Break. At first only a few came, but then it grew. Those who came told others; mostly it seems it spread through dog owners talking about it while exercising their dogs in the nearby park! We ran the group; Joy took a major role.

> At first it was a drop-in centre, but developed into more of a club. Joy left and another person took over, not a church member. In the beginning we had a number of outside speakers, but not so many now. Those who come often take turns to speak about their own life experiences. They run the club themselves. We have had to learn to let go.

The visual group summed it up with diagrams and a few words:

US

US and THEM

WE

Uncovering the story

Telling the story was easy and energized folk. Reflecting was harder. Not hard to keep the conversation going, but enabling it to go a bit deeper than reminiscing. Two aspects that were 'uncovered' were the importance of enabling ownership and, conversely, letting go. There were, we were told, other clubs in the area run by the social services for the elderly, but Tuesday Tea Break was different; it is a club run by its own members. As a result, it has become a catalyst for other self-motivated initiatives such as 'Golden Girls', a small entertainment group now much in demand. This kind of 'empowering' and 'owning' has only come about as church members have been willing to let go. That had not always been easy.

A different perspective

At this point we were running out of time, but there was just time to begin to look from a different perspective. We chose to use the Bible here; other ways would also be appropriate. The 'letting go' reflection had prompted the questions: Was it worthwhile? What was it all about? Only one person had become a regular church member as a result. At this point we worked in two groups again. Each group had to brainstorm and see what Bible passages came to mind that might help at this point. The list we made included:

- Jesus eats and drinks with all sorts

- God's plan to bring everyone together (Ephesians)

- Peter's vision of animals in a sheet. For **everyone**

- Salt and light and yeast

- Jesus letting go. Spirit there, after Jesus has gone

We were running out of time because we were all so caught up in the process that it was hard to move things on, so we had our own tea break!

Deepening or giving value to

Time being short we curtailed the process at this stage. The idea had been to plan a short liturgy to close the morning, instead we decided to plan the morning service for the following day, drawing on our work together. This brought forth a number of ideas and further discussion on the value of being salt and light in the community. Those present were convinced about the importance of this; some others in church apparently were not. We wanted to use the tea break story to raise further awareness. How to do this?

'Start with a cup of tea…', someone suggested. This was not so unusual at St B's and it was agreed to offer everyone a cup of tea when they arrived. Ideas then flowed. We would include 'telling the story', some of the scripture passages (several short readings with Taizé music in the background) and John was asked to give a short reflection. We also wanted to involve the congregation and so decided to give out local newspapers and ask those present to work in small groups and look for articles that spoke about needs in the community. These were then to be cut out and, as part of the intercessions, formed into a cross.

Sunday morning came and a congregation of about forty; a good number of St B's. All went according to plan. Well, almost, 'No tea. Thank you dear, I don't want to have to go to the loo', two elderly women told me. 'And I've been working all night and now you want me to do something', grumbled a young woman when confronted with newspaper and scissors. Mostly, however, there was great excitement about the service. 'One of the best…'. This was a communion service and the circle formed around the table embraced the cross made of the newspapers. 'That really spoke to me', said Sue.

In his 'little sermon' John had taken a glass of water and a packet of salt and demonstrated how salt disperses in the water. A child came and drank from the glass, saying 'Ugh' to the salty water. But the demonstration spoke for itself; few words were needed. 'Is this not the kind of mission Jesus calls us to?' asked John. 'To be salt and light in our local community, or like leaven in a loaf of bread. To demonstrate God's presence; to be a catalyst.'

Earlier in the weekend Michael and I had joined Ron Ram for an informal evening with members of neighbourhood groups. 'It's all very well changing our model of church, but if the clergy haven't changed, where are we?' said Joy. This is a matter of grave concern for St B's because John retires in a few months. Others picked this up. 'It's no good our being put back five years.' 'We need to know we are not on our own, that we are wanting to "break out of the mould" together. Clergy need to be trained to be able to respond to all these changes.'

August 2001

A conversation with Joy Burrett has assured me that the members of St B's are in good heart. Some members of the congregation have moved on; new ones have come. The most significant move has been that the two congregations of St B's and St Michael's have moved closer as a result of the inter-regnum. (In 1998 John had become vicar of the United Benefice of St Michael's, Devonport, and St Barnabas; neighbourhood groups had formed there too, as in St Bs.) The two churches now have a paid pastoral administrator and meet for joint worship preparation and also have a joint social committee. I remembered on our last visit the buzz about social events: 'We'll have a lot in the interregnum. It will be important to keep meeting together as a church.'

Joint worship preparation is a time of looking ahead at the lectionary readings, reflecting on them, choosing themes and appropriate hymns. At St B's visiting clergy come twice a month, preach and consecrate the elements; the service itself is led by members of the congregation. On the other two Sundays morning praise is led wholly by members. All these changes are making it easier for the small congregation to run the church efficiently. The neighbourhood groups have been merged into one core group for the time being; another simpli-fication. Support continues for community projects. These mostly run themselves; the Tuesday Tea Break is growing in numbers.

The 'barn of a church' is still conveniently standing, but there is, Joy told me, the possibility that something might happen quite quickly now. What has not yet happened is a suitable applicant to fill the post of team minister. Perhaps, thought Joy, the task is too daunting, the area itself uninviting, 'I suppose in a way we can run the church quite happily ourselves,' Joy confessed, 'but we do need someone alongside to move things on a bit. Someone who can realize where we're at and work with us to develop that.'

20

What and who is the church? Zion Baptist Church in Cambridge

I had hoped to visit Zion Baptist Church on my first journey, but this did not work out. I had, however, heard Tony Barker, minister of Zion Baptist Church, tell its story at High Leigh in January 1999. Afterwards I asked him if he would write the story down for a New Way booklet, *A Tapestry of Stories*. I include an edited version here. The story is of 'being church in the community seven days a week, twenty-four hours a day'.

Tony Barker's story, 1999

It all began with the Friday free community lunch. Two of the members had long dreamt of offering a free lunch to the city, so in the autumn of 1994, one Friday, they took pilchard sandwiches, made a pot of tea, opened the doors of the church hall and prayed, 'Lord, thank you for all the guests that you will bring along.' No one arrived. The two were dejected. Just as they were closing the doors an old man, Ken, looked in. 'What are you doing?' he asked. They explained. 'Bloody silly idea,' said Ken, 'nobody will come.'

The next Friday, pilchard sandwiches, a pot of tea and prayer but still no one came. Until at the end of the hour Ken looked in. 'I told you no one would come', he said triumphantly. 'But you have come', they said.

The third week Ken was waiting for the doors to open. Now regularly each week there are forty to fifty guests. The meals remain free of charge and most of the food is donated. Crowds of people turn up to help. More than 13,000 meals have been served to a wide cross-section of the city community, including homeless people, students, office workers and the mayors of Cambridge. This simple meal has lived the biblical injunction to *practise hospitality*; its effects have been great in the city.

Zion Baptist Church was, and still is, a tiny church. True, it has a huge building erected in 1879, but the number of people is very small. In the early 1900s there had been discussion about closing the church building and the congregations dispersing. Set in the centre of the city and once surrounded by hundreds of family houses, long demolished, the church faced a desperate situation. Many of the members of the church had left for the large and more flourishing churches in the city. A fragile, weak and fearful group were left, with little hope but to hang on and pray.

Elsewhere, and independently, God was prompting six people to consider moving to Zion, with a specific vision for the local community. If there has been any *new way of being church,* it is due to the divine Spirit of a loving God and a sense of desperation in the people. In autumn 1994 a new vision came to the church which focused on the surrounding community. There were many problems associated with the centre of the city, and the church located its mission in that centre, seeking to pray and live 'your kingdom come' rather than 'may our church grow'. So community mission has become the heart of the church.

First, the call of God came to six, then to other individuals, usually without any human prompting. Over five years, hundreds of visitors have come to visit the church and its projects, sometimes just to look and ask what the Lord is doing. Others have stayed wanting to participate in a tiny community that has dedicated itself to the poor and often marginalized, where the living presence of Christ has been discovered in a new way. The strength of the core group has been in its smallness and reliance on God.

While the Friday lunch already mentioned was developing, other projects were starting. Three examples are given:

- Contact was made with surrounding institutions, including the next-door-neighbour Anglia Polytechnic University. The church had long rented its hall to the university for orchestra practice, as a commercial venture. The suggestion was made to the APU that a creative partnership could be established as a model of community in the city. The University responded warmly to the idea and now includes the church on its campus plan. A redundant basement room in the church was refurbished by the APU and set aside as a quiet room for students and staff of any faith. All graduation ceremonies are now held in the Zion Chapel and special services, lectures and musical events are also welcomed.

- Like many city communities in Britain, there were a number of homeless people sleeping rough on the streets of Cambridge. The Zion church identified another huge area of its basement which had long been derelict, and decided to turn it into a night shelter. Jimmy's Nightshelter opened in December 1995 and has provided more than 55,000 bed places for some very special people who would otherwise have slept in the car parks and shop doorways. Opening at 7 pm every night of the year, Jimmy's provides hot meals, good clean beds, washing facilities and advocacy services for housing, justice and health.

- One gospel project leads to another. Cambridgeshire Social Services and the City Council asked the church to begin a community transport scheme, 'because we have seen how your church cares for people'. Research had discovered that there were about 7,000 people in the city who could not use public transport due to physical disability. Cambridge Dial a Ride has now been operating for five years and has purchased six buses with plans for two more, providing 13,600 journeys. A very committed staff team with some volunteer drivers and office helpers provide mobility to 630 members, many of whom would be confined to their homes without Dial a Ride.

New opportunities are presenting themselves all the time. The Cambridge Institute of Urban Community Mission was founded in January 1999 to reflect theologically on the projects and give other people an opportunity to think about God in the context of Zion and its life. Visitors have come from all over Britain, and now other countries, to learn and comment.

The small Zion church community, which has come to understand church as seven days a week, twenty-four hours a day, has learned to trust God in a new way. Sunday is one day to remember the miracles and hear the testimonies, as well as offering support and prayer for the projects. The sense of God's possibilities, rather than the church's strength, is ever present.

Update, 2001

Since the above was written an assessment has been made of the three years in which Zion Baptist Church has been accompanied by a BBH participant observer. In this case too, it was Ron Ram. Picked out for comment is the emphasis that Zion has placed on projects and therefore the challenge to the very nature of 'church'. 'How many members does Zion Baptist Church have?' was a question asked. The answer proffered was, 'Well, there are over 250 project volunteers.' The report continues:

> This concept raises some interesting conflicts and questions about the traditional perception of the Church, Christianity and belief.
>
> Why don't these 250+ 'church members' worship with the church on Sundays? Perhaps worship is something which can be more inherently practical and carried out while driving a bus, or at Jimmy's 'while washing feet' instead?

Knowing something of the background of Zion's project volunteers: how do we react to the implication that some of our 'church members' are Buddhists, Muslims, perhaps agnostics or even atheists?

These, the writer acknowledges, are challenging questions. They are questions to do with life and movement. Zion Baptist Church is now committed to take this process further as part of Stage C of BBH.

21

Reflections: Engaging with the world

The two churches whose stories are told in this section are both evangelical churches – evangelical churches that have come to a new way of understanding gospel, salvation, Bible, church. Such new understandings come, I believe, when one is faced with what is different, new, real. I am back, I realize, to where I started these reflections after my first journey. It brings to mind an experience from my days working as a youth leader in south London, I went to my first job as girls' club leader full of zeal to make converts, but I was the one who was converted. My whole outlook on life changed by experiencing a different reality from my comfortable middle-class upbringing.

The overall purpose of BBH is 'to explore what ways of being church enable local Christian communities to join effectively in the mission of God – with others'. The focus is the world, not the church.

Pauline, another member of the New Way team, tells how one Sunday morning there was a Fun Run for charity in the village in Essex where she lived. She was late driving to church and when she came to the village she saw she would have difficulty reaching the church. People were everywhere, lining the road to watch the runners pass. All the village organizations were supporting the run; it was bringing the village together. 'But where are we Christians?' thought Pauline. 'In church, with our backs to all of it!' She stayed to watch the run. Her priorities were challenged that day.

Only as we engage fully with the world around can appropriate new forms of ministry, worship and nurture emerge. It is the only way.

Signs of life

22

What kind of church?

Old and new

I have told how during my visit to Llansantffraid ym Mechain I stumbled unexpectedly over my own roots in Welsh chapel life. There were other roots I unexpectedly stumbled over too. During the introductions I was asked questions about the Fisherfolk and where all of them were now. The Fisherfolk were a ministry of the Community of Celebration, a ministry team well-known in the UK in the 70s and 80s for teaching on renewal in worship. Here on the Welsh borders I discovered that they are still remembered with affection and gratitude. Later Lyn Rogers himself wrote to explain the relationship in greater detail, the connections with the present story.

'The roots of the Llansantffraid Llanfechain story are found,' he wrote, 'in the whole theology and spirituality of the Community of Celebration, where I first realized my deep hope that it was possible for the Acts of the Apostles to be worked out in modern parish life.' He went on to share about the impact of a course on life and relationships in the body of Christ entitled *Expressing His Life*, a publication of the Community of Celebration at Post Green. There was, he said, a profound connection between present events and the concept of 'givenness' learnt from doing this course. As a result, in more recent years 'it would appear we were as a church flying some kind of flag which made it possible and easy for disparate groups of people to approach us'.

The Post Green Community – a Community of Celebration in the 1980s of which I was a member – came into being as a part of the charismatic renewal. The Community of Celebration, with its beginnings in the Church of the Redeemer, Houston, Texas, USA, was similarly influenced by the charismatic renewal. Both communities are still in existence but smaller. The young women and men who made up the Fisherfolk teams are scattered across the world. But for me to hear all this now, ten or more years on, has been fascinating and immensely encouraging. It is also a reminder of the deep roots of any renewal or movement of change within the Church.

What is shared in the journeys in this book is new and yet not new. It has a new expression in our day, but its roots are in what has gone before. There is solidity together with surprise. Many of us can look back over our lives and see how the threads intertwine; how we too have had our lives moulded and shaped by such movements of the Spirit, and have also helped to shape.

Prompted, I expect, by the above experiences, I found myself thinking often on my journeys of conversations with Graham Pulkingham, an Episcopal priest and founder of the Community of Celebration, and of his writings. I felt he had expressed so much of what I was experiencing, had put it into words. Yet Graham had died in 1994 of a heart attack; he knew nothing of BBH. Back home I pulled out a book, *Renewal: An Emerging Pattern*, published by Celebration in 1980, and read a contribution by Graham on 'the shape of the church to come'. Part of the introduction to this book reads:

> Graham Pulkingham contends for a 'sociology of the body of Christ that does not separate it from its root in the body of Adam'. He sees the term the 'body of Christ' as an analogy of Paul's to 'illuminate the condition of Jesus' continuing spiritual presence known and felt as a hearthside – homely, commonplace – because his life and mission are continued, his value and point of view are fostered by the full-bodied existence of his followers in every walk of life.' How else can Christ's presence be felt in the world?

Hearthside – that was the word I had dimly remembered. This

is close to the concept of a kitchen space, a phrase that is found often in BBH papers.

> In our own sharing of stories we have learned again and again of the importance of the kitchen as a safe space in a house, where the most ordinary things go on, in which anybody can be invited to join and from which flow friendship, understanding and trust.

'How many of our churches have the space which allows for this?' is the question asked by the Value Sharing Project.

Simon Barrington-Ward, later Bishop of Coventry, in a Foreword to *Renewal: An Emerging Pattern,* find echoes in Graham Pulkingham's writings of Charles Péguy, the great Catholic poet and mystic of the late nineteenth century. 'Péguy', Simon Barrington Ward wrote, 'passionately yearned to see restored the true "parish", a symbol to him of a church rooted in the whole of man's actual world; not withdrawn into false piety, but pervaded with a profound power of intercession and mediation.'

If we were to chase the roots of what is now growing newly in our day, we would chase them all the way back to the first Christian community and beyond. We are in good company.

What kind of space?

I have shared that my time in Heath Town ended on a sad note indeed: the news that an aunt had died. She was a very special aunt, a person who had always been there for me, a close friend, and her death was hard to handle. I had to put this book aside, reschedule my third journey and with my cousins concentrate on all the arrangements that follow such a bereavement. I write about this now because the experience also reaffirmed for me so much that is good and positive about the church – particularly in its pastoral role, a role that is an inestimable gift to people in times of crisis, as well as in times of celebration. This pastoral role is often a hidden one, taken for granted maybe. 'Not always done well', a friend reminded me. No, not always, but often. I am grateful to the clergy and others who were there for me and other members of the family this summer and 'did it well'. I have found it helpful to keep this experience in mind as I have explored other reflections about church, more critical perhaps.

It is almost September as I write these final reflections on my journeys. Yesterday I met up with a friend and told her about this book. She then began to talk about her own local church – Methodist. 'We have many house groups', she said. 'Not all those who belong come to church on Sundays. The group is their church, I guess. Things have changed a lot in that way.' Her remark was quite unsolicited, and very apt. I was taken by surprise, because I had not expected her matter-of-factness. A new shape is already here. Radical change is like that, often creeping up on you unawares. House groups, interest groups, neighbourhood groups, action groups, they are all a part of this new shape of church. Groups have, of course, been around a long while, but often as an 'extra', not as a basic unit of church. My journeying has, however, broadened my ideas still further about where I expect to meet church. Visiting the Club in Edinburgh I picked up the phrase 'offering a variety of spaces' to enable people in different situations and contexts a place of meaning or exploration – church. That image of a 'variety of spaces' is expressive of so much I have heard and experienced on these journeys. It is untidy, but it offers such hope. It makes sense of much that I and others are currently experiencing, of the many different spaces initiated or found to explore faith and meaning. I mentioned these in my reflections on my third journey. All the places visited during these past four months are offering just such spaces: pop-in clubs, cafés, community centres, and homes too.

One essential element in all these 'spaces' is that they are not offering answers but enabling exploration. A friend of mine found that she had many questions following the death of a close friend, and then discovered that her local church could not help her here; indeed, it discouraged their exploration. To be true to her own journey she had to find another 'space' which would enable such exploration. The space she found was in the academic world in pursuing a doctorate in spirituality. There she has found new friends and a different kind of support – 'church'?

Theological reflections following a 'What is Church Consultation' held at High Leigh in January 1999 are helpful here.

'Is it enough simply to call oneself church? Is it enough to believe that "when two or three are gathered together in my name, I am there among them"? Is there a theological bottom line provided from some outside authority, or can we let a thousand or more flowers bloom, flourish or die without compunction?' asks Dr Anne Richards, the Church of England's Mission Theology Secretary, in her paper following the Consultation.

Later in this paper, she suggests that 'One way we can get at the question *What is church*? is to see the church as "framing the question".' In this way 'we can see the search for theological understanding and the desire for value, meaning and purpose as missiological, driving the Church continuously into being, and indeed, into remaking itself.' She then cites as a result expressions emerging in prisons, trains, classrooms and perhaps even in committees. 'The question is then how these incipient forms of church contribute to "framing the question". How they open up fresh insight into God's ultimate intention for creation...'

What is this word church anyway? In New Way workshops we like to explore the original meaning of such words; they hint at important truths, often overlooked. Peter Price, Anglican Bishop of Kingston, a member of the New Way team, writes in one of our booklets:

> The term Church is usually associated with a religious gathering; although sometimes political parties and other groups describe themselves as 'broad church'. This is interesting because the word church was a secular term in the Greek and Roman empires. It means

a gathering, a meeting or more precisely – a gathering of the called out, or elected ones. In the Roman Empire the term ecclesia or church had a particular association with community organising. A church was a gathering of free citizens (the elected ones) whose task was to seek the welfare of the neighbourhood.

If a secular term was used to describe the Early Church, what words might be applied now? Café, centre, college – perhaps just the phrase 'a space'?

What is apt?

I was expecting to collect on my journeys examples of new forms of worship, ways of integrating Scripture and life. Mostly I was disappointed here, an unexpected gap. Sometimes my questions about this area seemed to take people by surprise. It was not that prayer or regular times of worship didn't happen, but in form and style little, it seemed, had changed here in contrast to other areas. My visit to each place was, of course, short – a few hours or a day at most – so this is an impression only. I am, however, confident that here is a major opportunity for exploration. Here we can learn much from the example of basic ecclesial communities.

Scripture is central to the life of these communities; an integration of Bible and life. Carlos Mesters, a Dutch Catholic missionary and Carmelite priest, writes of the Brazilian experience:

> In the people's lives the Bible and life are connected. When they open the Bible they want to find in it things directly related to their lives, and in their lives they want to find events and meanings that parallel those in the Bible. Spontaneously they use the Bible as an image, symbol, or mirror of what is happening to them here and now.

There are three aspects to this way of reading the Bible – the Bible itself, people's daily reality and the life of the Christian community or cell. Learning to relate to the Bible in this way is an essential element of our New Way of Being Church workshops. Bishop Peter Price has also developed a series of New Way booklets based on the Gospels, which bring Bible, community and reality together in this way. These follow readings from the common lectionary and are an aid for small church groups. Peter Price writes in a booklet on such interactive learning:

> I strongly hold the view that in order for God to be heard speaking and seen to be acting today, three things are needed. First, accepting and dealing with the reality of everyday life, warts and all. Second, recognising the need to be part of community, both intentional, like a house or neighbourhood group, as well as a given community such as a street, apartment block or neighbourhood. Third, the Bible.

'Why does normal church life have so little sharing of our stories in our worship?' is a principal finding of the Value Sharing Group. Indeed, it touches on 'the foremost finding of this group ... the innate value, significance and encouragement that comes from the opportunity to tell and share our respective stories.'

I think of a Sunday a few years back when I worshipped with a small congregation in the Netherlands. 'A basic Christian community of sorts' is how they described themselves; sharing about what they are doing is an integral part of their weekly worship. A typical example would be the Sunday that one member told of her experiences as a single parent dependent upon social security allowance. Another member, who worked 'on the other side of the counter' in the social security office, talked about his work. 'How it is he does this job and his concern to be as human a possible in the way he does it.' This was the sermon slot.

Another story comes from nearer home, Magdalen Smith, an Anglican priest and a member of the New Way team, decided with some trepidation to try a new way of preaching – new

117

to her anyway – a dialogue-sermon. A previously apathetic congregation seemed to come to life. One week, after a reading about the widow's mite, Mags asked the question, 'What does sacrifice mean for you?' She later wrote down what happened:

> A variety of people spoke, and then there was a pause. I was about to continue when a voice I hadn't heard before spoke up. A woman, who had sat with her disabled sister at the back of the church regularly Sunday after Sunday, wanted to say something. Usually I think I was the only person she spoke to. 'Sacrifice, for me', Gilda said, 'has meant looking after Cathy here, my sister, all my life. Cathy fell down the stairs when she was quite young and hasn't been able to cope on her own ever since. None of my other family felt they could do this apart from me. I've never got married and I think it might be something to do with the way my life has been. Not that I mind or anything, this is just the way things are.'

Mags, reflecting on this experience later, wrote: 'I realize now that many people come to church week after week desperate to be able to share something like this, something of how their lives really are, and to be part of a group of people who will understand and support them.'

'Liturgy, if it is to be describe as "apt", needs to express people's deepest fear and hopes', says Ann Morisy, Ministry Adviser in the Anglican diocese of London, in her book *Beyond the Good Samaritan: Community Ministry and Mission.* 'The chief reason,' she writes,

> in terms of mission for inviting participation is that through it people will become open to experiences which resonate with their often unspoken awareness of issues of 'ultimate concern'. Through their commitment to a struggle which is wider than their own well-being, people are enabled to muse on the big questions of life. Does my life and the lives of those with whom I am

involved have any meaning? Does the world in which I am cast without my consent have any purpose? ... People have a hunger for meaning.

This matter of apt liturgy is, I believe, a key area of moving forward the process of 'changing church'. But there are skills and gifts involved, and time and energy. Those I met with from the Late Late Service talked about this. Fewer in number, they are having to cut back on the number of alternative worship events held on a regular basis. It raises the question of what kind of gifts and what resources are needed to enable such change.

What people development?

There was a vacancy for a new minister. The vacancy was for a congregation engaged in new forms of ministry in an inner-city context – a situation similar in many ways to several of those described in this book. A possible candidate emerged, but 'Would I have enough to do?' the candidate asked. The opening was to support a strong lay leadership and engagement with the local community. As far as I know the vacancy still exists. I discovered on these journeys that a number whose stories are told here are in this situation, or soon will be. There is not a lot of confidence around that these vacancies will be filled, or filled appropriately. It is a telling tale.

Such developments do not, as Martin Johnstone pointed out to me, rise or fall with the appointment of a minister. Or should not, but often it is a requirement. Yet there is a need for enabling gifts or ministries, and it seems there are far too few opportunities for appropriate training for lay or ordained members engaged in new models of church. One of my observations early on in these journeys concerned a lack of confidence expressed by lay members to engage in 'church' ministries – leading services or Bible study groups, for example. Work in the community was fine, but not 'church' ministry; they had not had the appropriate training. It raises

the image in my mind of large numbers of lay people supporting and enabling one ordained woman or man to engage
in the task of ministry as church in the world. It should be the
other way round!

Working among the many scattered villages of rural Lincolnshire, John Cole, Ecumenical Development Officer for Mission
and Unity, has come across a pattern of church members fully
engaged in their local communities, but not distinctively as
church. Part of his job is to 'build people's confidence in God
so that they are more distinctive while being no less engaged'.
This, John admits, involves a whole paradigm shift: the need
'to get away from depending on the clergy and from thinking
only in terms of the survival of the church as an institution'.
The task here is to enable these tiny Christian communities to
'become what they are' – local embryonic cells of church. John
Cole cites Robert Warren's *Building Missionary Congregations*:
'The whole-life focus of these village congregations needs to
be affirmed. What they need in their tiny locality is not the
dead weight of the traditional Vicar but the encouragement of
what Robert describes as a "facilitator".'

I knew that this question of ministry would surface many
times in my conversations during these months. I anticipated
lively debates and new insights arising from them about the
place of the ordained ministry in a changing church. This has
happened. I had not expected to see so clearly how changes in
perception and training have to be more all-encompassing. A
whole new pattern of ministry – both lay and ordained – is
called for and a quite new approach to training. Re-reading
my BBH papers, I find that this same emphasis is there. The
BBH Data Analysis Group stated:

> There has been very little response to the question,
> 'What people development is consciously taking place?'
> Most training is of a general nature and is not focused
> on how to deal with local practicalities. The data shows
> that the development of laity and clergy is mainly
> separate even though they are required to work
> together locally.

As a result it was apparently difficult to get lay people to contribute theologically to the BBH process and to participate in the sub-projects.

One place where programmes are currently being developed that bring lay and ordained members of a local church together for in-service training is the Urban Theology Unit (UTU) in Sheffield. I was given a bed for the night at UTU while visiting The Furnival, which gave me an opportunity to ask questions. UTU has helped to initiate and given continuing support to two places I had visited, Bellshill and The Furnival. That impressed me to begin with. Christine Jones, Director of Studies at UTU, told me of her concern about those currently entering the Methodist ministry: 'Several last year did not survive even one year in their new appointments.' It seems that the pressure for change is likely now to come from many different quarters. 'Where else in the country do you see new models of training emerging?' I asked Christine. There was a pregnant pause; she did not give me an answer.

The BBH 'Formation for Ministries' Sub-Project hinted in December 1999 that it too had found a lack of new initiatives across the country. However, in my journeys I have come across a number of less formal initiatives that are offering training and support in a variety of ways. I am thinking of Grassroots, UTU certainly, and the diocesan and ecumenical initiatives that I have mentioned. I would also include New Way, and also Sarum College, an ecumenical centre of Christian learning and spiritual growth, close to where I live in Dorset. In our New Way resources we have lists of different agencies and initiatives that have gifts to offer for the kind of development mentioned in this book. These initiatives are for the most part 'extras' to traditional ministerial and theological training. I believe that all of them have a part to play in shaping the future of the Church's ministry.

One thing that may be different here is that many of these initiatives are locally based and engaged in local ministry.

These local links seem to be an imperative, a part of engaging in what is 'real'. Again the Sub-Project Report on the Formation of Ministries picks this up:

> So we could have a situation where someone from a particular local situation, and who feels called to 'full-time' ministry is trained in such a way as continues to link them to their home situation, and perhaps involves the training of an identified lay team as training progresses.

The scene is wide open to many possibilities! What are important are the increasingly affirmed principles on enabling, the affirmation of a variety of gifts, and the focus on the local and on God's action in the whole world.

Is faith being shared?

A concern about whether faith sharing is an integral part of all these initiatives is acknowledged and addressed in reports produced by BBH. It is a question often asked by concerned member churches. A paper from the BBH Data Analysis Group recognizes that those associated with BBH take many different stances about mission. A common understanding, however, would be, 'God's mission is almost universally understood to be people-centred, so that as many as possible can know the love revealed in Jesus Christ and find faith.' But whether people are finding faith remains a key question.

Looking back over my journeys this summer, my gut response is 'yes'. Wherever I went I found people who are finding faith in a variety of different ways – in a new sense of their own self-worth, a new sense of respect and trust for others, belief in the future of their communities and what they themselves can contribute, and a new awareness that God is at work in their lives and in the world around them. Of course, what I found is not as neatly parcelled as that. I am stumbling to find words to express what I met. Words I shared in the third journey section come to mind, words written by a man without a home (see p. 35):

We're on a path from loneliness to friendship,
It isn't easy and the way is dark and long.
We try to love, respect and help each other.
Let's keep right on till the pathway ends.

These are words written to be sung at a worship time. They are real, they come from the heart, but they are not a traditional formulation of faith. They convey an experience; implicit in them is a new-found faith and meaning. Perhaps the challenge here is how we recognize faith. If we are looking for a traditional faith response we may be missing the real thing.

Meeting faith-sharing, often of this more untraditional kind, in the places I visited was not only moving, it encouraged my own faith. Mostly I simply stumbled across these expressions of faith – in stories, comments, a sentence or two spoken almost incidentally in the midst of all else that was going on; an expression of the whole activity of God in that place. People had found faith again, or were curious, or knew, they said, that God cared. In many places I sensed that enabling such faith to grow and be nurtured was more the challenge than the initial sharing and naming of God's activity. Where are the places – the churches if you will – that can provide appropriate nurture?

I think of my own experience, forty years back, working in open youth clubs in South London with mostly unchurched young people. It was also true then that engaging young people in conversation about God and church was never difficult. They brought the conversation round to the subject time and again. Some came to a personal faith, but the gap between them and institutional Church meant that other places needed to be found to nurture that faith. Then, we created a 'church in the club'; a similar response to today's. What, if anything, is different now from then? It does seem that now there is a new openness in the institutional Church to allowing itself to be challenged, changed, by this situation; a new sense of urgency, the compelling of the Spirit.

Churches, it seems, are caught between a rock and a hard

place. Numbers are leaving – not so much the Church, as traditional Sunday worship; others are looking for 'something' but find 'the Sunday thing' confusing and irrelevant. BBH's Data Analysis Group states: 'The fact that people do not come to church clearly indicates new ways of bringing Christians together with other people need to be found.'

What kind of ecumenism?

One way in which Christians are coming together is through networks. George Lings, who is associated with Anglican Church Planting Initiatives, talks about an 'emerging breed of network churches'. By this he means 'a church which has been deliberately set up, and officially authorized to work only with networks of people. Unlike a parish it has no exclusive area to call its own'. This move, he says, recognizes that numbers of people 'not only live their lives in networks of relationships, but find their identity through this'.

Networks or webs were key words for many of us in the 80s. A guided meditation often used in workshops comes to mind. In an attitude of prayer we imagined a web.

> The web extends beyond this room, for it is made up of relationships ... woven of the flows and interconnections that interlace you with the universe ... Experience now the great multiplicity of strands ... Relationships formed by the love and work and laughter and tears you've shared with other beings ... They extend across space, across time ... They shape what you are ... They sustain and give you place ...

I think of the many webs over the years that have helped to sustain and give me place. Some of these webs have proved more durable than intentional community, which is perhaps too static for today's society. All of them are grounded in relationships; friendship is a key element in kin-dom building. I think of how insistent Peter Harvey at The Furnival was about the importance of relationships. Networking, building partnerships, is about this: it is useful, resourceful, but more importantly it is about people laughing, struggling, envisioning; at best an expression of God's love.

In the 1980s we talked a lot about the concept and experienced it on a small scale. Now its potential is being realized in ways unthought of then. I have learnt a lot about partnership and networking on these journeys and been impressed by many kin-dom webs in place. A web is being spun that is drawing together aspects of life usually kept separate.

I have mentioned before the intentional community of which I was part in the 1970s and early 1980s. One impression that some people had towards the close of this period was indeed of a spider's web: an idea of dispersion – of going out into the world and indeed into many parts of the world (we already numbered 90 or so in all). We didn't understand this 'word' then – or chose not to do so, but today members are scattered all over the world. Perhaps more aptly, at Post Green a new initiative has been pioneered by the community: a centre which offers short stay accommodation primarily to people with disabilities and their carers. It is a secular organization which carries the ethos of the Post Green Community. It is – like many of the stories told in this book – a partnership between the secular and the spiritual. It is a place where the integration of disability, the arts, the environment and spirituality is being pursued, a holistic vision that Carolyn Reinhart, its Project Worker and formerly a member of the community, sees as in keeping with a modern quantum worldview that 'integrates our sense of self ... the environment as a whole, the planet, universe and God into some overall purpose or sense of direction'. It seems a far cry from where we began, with a narrower and almost wholly 'spiritual' vision, but God moves us on gently – or not so gently!

In this holistic kin-dom vision there is no place for discrimination on the grounds of sex or race or colour or age or any other 'or'. Here the word ecumenism might be used instead of networks or partnerships. During these journeys I have been impressed over and over again by the working ecumenism I have found. I cannot conceive these initiatives working in any other way. I learnt a new term while I was in Brazil visiting basic Christian communities in 1997: *grassroots ecumenism*. This term could equally well be used about the stories told here – an ecumenism growing from local necessity. In Brazil this necessity has been to come together with neighbours of other faiths. An Anglican priest, Peter Cotton, attending a similar gathering in 2000, wrote in a New Way newsletter:

> a bold vision of ecumenism. At a Great Mass for a Land without Evils, the Catholic Bishops were joined not only by leaders of Protestant Churches but also by priestesses of the Afro-Brazilian cults and leaders of the indigenous people with their traditional religion. To receive a parting blessing from all of these together was a blessing indeed and spoke of the common humanity with which our destructive inhumanity has to be confronted.

The explosive interest today in spirituality is going to spin off more webs – in academia, in commerce, in medicine and education, in environmental awareness. The pace of change is fast. Are we ready for this?

What of the future?

'What is the church of our dreams?' In New Way workshops we ask participants to draw both the church of their dreams and also 'the church as they experience it'. They do this first individually and then in groups of four or more. Following this the drawings are pinned up so that similarities and difference can be noted and reflected on. Invariably the drawings have a startling similarity – the movement in the 'dreams' drawings is always outward into the world and often depicts the church as dispersed in the community in small cells or units. Sometimes we pin alongside these drawings posters showing the global make-up of basic christian communities – a new way of being church. Always we are amazed at the striking similarity: the dream of such a church seems to be universal.

The dream is there – something coming from the heart – but it is not always easy to translate into action. For most who come to the workshops one small step towards the dream is all that is possible in their present situation. The stories in this book are the exception rather than the rule. Yet here too there is fragility, uncertainty, vulnerability. Some of the projects are at risk. Certainly they are places that need resourcing and support – the right kind of support. As tantalizing models of what can be, they press us to go further – to risk, to make the radical changes that are implied, necessary, urgent.

'We want to say that the church needs to choose life...'. An open letter to an Anglican bishop starts with these words. It continues,

> we have too often found the official church to be a barrier rather than a bridge of hope. ... The world is changing rapidly ... We believe the church is in a good position to resource and fund schemes which allow people, clergy and lay, to be set free to act as catalysts of change, as networkers, as social entrepreneurs and community development workers. ... The church still has resources and influence and must not squander them on the unreal world of a closed institution. So our message to the church is 'get real'.

Is then something substantive happening, a reformation, a paradigm shift? It was heartening to me to hear Martin Johnstone say that he believes there is now a much greater opportunity of this happening than at other times. 'Christendom no longer exists as it did once. It opens up the way for a truly new direction.' But he went on to say that the new models of church in which we are now engaging may themselves be provisional and will give way to others perhaps even more radical in shape; we are living in a transitional period as society.

Following that conversation I came across an article in the June 2001 issue of *Communities Australia* by Geraldine Leonard, a minister of the Uniting Church in Australia. She too wrote about the 'in-between times':

History tells us that the sorts of change we are currently undergoing can be hundreds of years before the old is completely gone and the new has fully emerged. Most of us don't have that long and so it seems wise to equip people for the 'in-between times'. To carefully craft a spirituality which equips people for a life of uncertainty...

She gives the Celtic church as a model of a church which thrived in a time of great change.

Where does the energy and the hope come from? How is it kept alive? I think back to where I started this book, to that word *yearning*. The something coming from the heart, that is not going to go away.

Appendix 1

A summary of Building Bridges of Hope and the action–research 'pilots' process

Simon Barrow

1. What is the aim and purpose of BBH?

The *aim* of Building Bridges of Hope (BBH) is **to discover what different ways of relating to local communities are most effective for mission** – mission being God's purposes for human community declared in Jesus Christ. BBH is a 'living laboratory' of different church initiatives. It is designed to work with the churches locally and nationally to discover 'best practice' for moving from maintenance to mission. It is therefore about implementing:

- creative ways of building bridges within and between communities

- new ways of being church that *connect to the local context*, and

- appropriate patterns of local mission, alongside others.

This requires:

- Making fresh connections between community, church and mission.

The overall *purpose* of this phase of BBH is **action–research for a changing church in a changing world**.

2. What is the BBH approach and how is it helpful?

- BBH is concerned with helping to **discern God's activity** in the world as well as in the church. Faith and hope is shared best in growing relationships.

- The BBH ethos is to **build change from the ground up**, not from the top down.

- BBH's hallmarks are **faith, innovation, learning, risk, linkages** and **synergy**.

- BBH is not a one-size-fits-all 'package' competing with the wares of others, but a shared **learning process** adaptable for each place.

- BBH is concerned to work across **different Christian traditions** in both 'inherited' and 'emergent' ways. It attracts those who have not worked together before.

- People involved in BBH have a **common commitment** to Jesus Christ. But they **understand mission in different ways** – as direct witness, personal faith commitment, social solidarity and/or sacramental presence, for instance.

- BBH is concerned with the **quality of church life** and its **connectedness to the wider community**. It is also concerned with **growth** that reflects these values.

- The BBH vision is realized wherever BBH can be linked with the ideas and projects of others to create **added value for all** concerned.

- The BBH philosophy is that **resources must be 'grown' locally** as the project changes and develops.

3. What has happened so far?

- In Stage A of Building Bridges of Hope (BBH) there was extensive visiting of diverse local churches, which led to consultation among the national churches; this confirmed the value of and commitment to a locally focused project to discern practical ways for churches to move from maintenance to mission; from self-engagement to more effective engagement with their local communities.

- In Stage B some 40 local places (churches of every type across Britain and Ireland) were accompanied, observed and researched over a three-year period as they sought to do this. Seven key learning factors emerged (see section 4).

- A small number of church-related community projects across North-West Europe also came together to look at gospel values in action.

- The BBH project has been 'incubated' by the churches in an ecumenical process through CTBI's Churches' Commission on Mission.

- The Association of Building Churches (ABC) is a new self-development network among those who have been involved to date. It is working at local level (see Key contacts, p. 142)

- The *Bridges to Build* video and D-I-Y workbook have been produced for the broadest range of local groups.

- A new rolling programme of action–research pilot projects has been launched to show how mission can be done in a changing world.

- BBH resource material is available on the web (www. ctbi.org.uk/bbh), through the forthcoming CTBI Lent Course 2002.

- BBH is seeking direct ownership by the churches locally and nationally over the next few years, and further collaboration with other agencies and initiatives.

4. What has been learned to date?

From a mass of evidence gathered in Stage B, seven key factors enabling local Christian communities to engage effectively in the mission of God in contemporary society have been identified, as follows:

1. **Focusing vision**. The importance of local churches articulating their specific calling through integrated strategies for community engaging, mature spiritual life, enabling leadership and appropriate structure.

2. **Building local partnerships**. The significance of seeking and forming partnerships of action with those with similar concerns in the wider community inside and outside the Church.

3. **Sharing faith and values**. A commitment to exploring respectful and creative ways to share values, aspirations and faith in and beyond church circles in relation to the gospel story.

4. **Nourishing daily living**. The critical need for believers old and new to relate biblical faith to personal life, work and culture in society today through worship and reflection.

5. **Developing shared leadership**. The importance of forming *in context* (clergy–lay and other forms of) team leadership, animated by one another and linked both to church learning institutions and to genuine community participation.

6. **Becoming communities of learning**. Churches at every level need to become places where the lessons about how to be 'bridge-builders' with others can be developed, consolidated and extended.

7. **Willingness to be accompanied**. The value of welcoming systematic accompaniment and evaluation in non-directive ways from beyond the local – and the networking of stories and experience in order to be able to look at each other with fresh eyes.

These are the seven 'learning indicators' that BBH will be carrying forward from Stage B to Stage C and testing in wider, innovative contexts. They connect strongly to what is being learned elsewhere among the churches at the moment. (The detailed research is described in the report *God's Mission and* the *Local Church*, available from the Churches' Commission on Mission (CCOM) – downloadable at www.ctbi.org.uk/bbh.)

5. What is the new action–research 'piloting' process?

Stage B of BBH was about drawing lessons from detailed observation of a variety of churches with different models of mission and no prior claim to being especially 'successful'. The idea was to look at a broad range of experiences, not to decide in advance what might 'work'. Effectiveness was to be determined in context.

In Stage C the aim is to focus on a narrower range of church situations ('pilots') that start from, but extend beyond, the 'local'. These will be places where initiatives are already under way – they will not be ideas or activities imposed from outside.

The pilots will include initiatives in dioceses, deaneries, provinces, churches together bodies, projects, action zones, experimental groups and training institutions: wherever the action is, or can be.

6. What are the aims of this 'piloting'?

The BBH pilots will be doing the following:

A. **Testing ideas**. Aiming to look at how the seven 'BBH learning indicators' can be developed, modified and applied in greater depth, in different settings, and in different combinations.

B. **Supporting initiative**. Aiming to assist the development of a network of support for ground-up initiatives in new ways of being and living church, for the sake of the world and in the light of the gospel.

C. **Challenging institutions**. Aiming to discover ways in which the resources, structures and agencies of 'the wider church' (denominationally and ecumenically) can be encouraged to enable, rather than block, mission initiatives arising from the ground-up.

D. **Breaking barriers**. Aiming to demonstrate new ('pioneering', 'emergent', 'developmental') ways forward in bridge-building and mission for local, regional and national churches.

7. What is the scope of BBH 'piloting'?

The intention is to have a 'rolling programme' of pilots in England, Scotland, Ireland and Wales, starting with a small, sustainable group (13 or more in Britain and Ireland by early 2002, plus further pilots in the other nations as soon as feasible) and then expanding further as resources become available. The pattern will vary across the nations.

Over a period of 2–5 years it is hoped that a broad range of pilots will be accompanied. These will reflect a variety of overall balances:

- different church traditions

- 'emergent' and 'inherited' situations

- age/gender/ethnic/social composition

- geographical spread

- urban/suburban/rural

- scale of operation

- plural/homogeneous character and style.

The result will be the beginnings of a 'living laboratory' for the churches in Britain and Ireland concerning different, effective ways of doing Christian mission across a range of contexts and factors.

8. What will BBH offer the 'pilots'?

BBH will seek to offer five things to those who become pilots:

- **ideas** to test and develop (arising from Stage B)
- skilled, sensitive and disciplined **accompaniment**/reflection
- developing **networking** with other innovators/developers
- **signposting** to other sources of support (training, consultancy)
- **recognition** as part of an ecumenical experiment in new ways of doing mission.

Such elements need to be generated collaboratively. Some will come from the small, existing BBH network, some from other local and national church sources. Opportunities will be sought for combining or sharing with different Christian agencies. Some resources are available through the ecumenical Churches' Commission on Mission – a consultant, a small budget and communications facilities. But fresh resources will need to be generated as the pilot project moves forward.

9. How will the 'pilots' be selected?

Throughout 2001 two part-time BBH development consultants have been working extensively across Britain and Ireland with church partners to discover initiatives which:

- Identify with the ground-up ethos of BBH and some or all of the 'seven learning indicators' (see section 4, above).
- Are engaged in a practical piece of innovation or development aimed at discovering new ways of being church and building bridges in society.
- Wish to be accompanied, observed, networked, linked and profiled over a period of 18 months to 2+ years as they develop (see section 8, above).
- Reflect some of the initial balances identified (see section 7, above), including 'ordinariness' (i.e. not just 'special projects').

The BBH Development Group, which comprises representatives of the churches locally and nationally, has guided the initial selection in view of the needs of the potential pilots themselves and with an eye to the more comprehensive range of situations it hopes to include in the longer run.

The action–research pilot process will look like a funnel that starts narrow and gets taller and wider as it is extended outwards.

The full list of 'pilots' is available from the Churches' Commission on Mission of Churches Together in Britain and Ireland.

10. How will 'piloting' work in practice?

Allowing for some variation across the nations, there are a number of stages to becoming a pilot:

1. After initial consultation and discussion an agreement will be drawn up between BBH and the potential pilot.

2. By mutual arrangement an accompanier will be identified – and will form a contract with both the pilot and BBH, after shared briefing and equipping.

3. The accompaniment will take place over a suitable period of time, most usually 18 months to two and a half years. Meetings between the accompanier and the pilot will take place at most every 8 weeks.

4. Pilots and accompanier will build up together, through discussion and questioning, a developing 'case study' and profile of what is being done and learned.

5. There will be a common framework for discussion and questioning (based on the seven learning indicators), but also much scope for variation according to context.

6. The pilots will be put in touch with each other and given opportunities to cluster, meet and share ideas and information.

7. Accompaniers and the network will identify other sources of practical support, often through agency, denominational and ecumenical bodies.

8. The accompaniers will be networked together for support, learning and sharing of discoveries (within agreed boundaries of confidentiality).

9. Pilots, accompaniers and (by agreement) church leaders and mission enablers may have the opportunity to participate in (probably bi-annual) residential 'Future Church' conferences. These will be places where the case studies are examined, pilots and observers can share their discoveries, and wider practical/reflective discussion can take place on opportunities and challenges for mission today.

10. As part of this whole process, ideas and stories will be shared with other interested parties well beyond BBH – especially through the Internet.

11. Channels for conversation with leaders and agencies will be identified on an ongoing basis aimed at making the insights of this project available for the wider Church.

12. There will be variations in this process as it is taken forward in England, Scotland, Ireland and Wales. The idea is to operate in an appropriately devolved way.

11. How will 'accompaniers' function?

Accompaniers will be chosen by the responsible BBH group in each of the four nations and in agreement with the pilots. A network of potential accompaniers is evolving. Their role alongside pilots will primarily involve:

- **Listening** (staying with the agenda of the pilot)

- **Questioning** (identifying key concerns within a common framework)

- **Reflection** (feeding back impressions and observations)

- **Discussion** ('helping to unblock thought')

- **Signposting** (pointing to other sources of specific help)

- **Interpretation** (building up a shared picture and case study)

- **Facilitation** (being an enabler).

This role involves participation as well as observation, but needs to recognize some boundaries over training and consultancy, which will need to be understood and agreed on both sides.

Qualities required beyond what is implied by the role outlined above include those of discretion, confidentiality and the ability to work and share in a team of accompaniers.

Accompaniers will be paid travel and out-of-pocket expenses on an agreed basis and will operate creatively but accountably (both to BBH and to the pilots they are contracted to). They will be supported, appraised and networked. They will benefit from the accumulation of experience, analysis and wisdom built up through the BBH network.

12. What outcomes can be expected from the 'pilots'?

The intended outcomes will be developed, defined and agreed as part of the contracting process, but they will definitely include:

- Identifiable benefits in learning, confidence and attainment for the pilots and the observers.

- Stories, ideas and models which can be shared in and beyond the BBH project (examples and stories of good practice).

- New insights for the churches concerning the practice of mission today and the orientation of church resources and structures to that end.

- Effective links and collaboration with other similar or complementary initiatives, including a network of accompaniers across Britain and Ireland.

- Growing ownership of BBH by the churches locally and nationally, and growing resources to accompany these developments.

Appendix 2

Resources

Bridges to Build is a 29-minute video, accompanied by a work booklet, aimed at local churches and mission enablers. The package costs £13.99 plus £2 postage and packing from: CTBI Publications, Great Smith Street, London SW1P 3BN. Tel. 020 7898 1300, fax 020 7898 1305; or order securely from the web at www.chbookshop.co.uk. Please do *not* order through CCOM.

The full Stage B (local congregations) report is called *God's Mission and the Local Church*. It can also be downloaded free from the website, or ordered in print for £10.00 from CCOM, Inter-Church House, 35–41 Lower Marsh, London, SE1 7SA. Tel. 020 7523 2121, fax 020 7928 0010. This material will soon be available on CD-ROM. Watch the website for details.

Other material, including the *BBH Values Project Report*, will go up on the BBH website (www.ctbi.org.uk/bbh) from time to time. We will be seeking to use the web as an information source as much as possible to save both costs and the environment!

The 2002 CTBI ecumenical Lent course, *Called to Be Saints*, includes BBH material. Visit the CTBI website for information: www.ctbi.org.uk/publications.

We also recommend the report by David Hay and Kate Hunt, *Understanding the Spirituality of People who Don't Go to Church*, which can be downloaded free from www.ccom.org.uk.

Other organizations

Catholic Missionary Society, www.cms.org.uk

Evangelism site, www.evangelism.uk.net

Grassroots, 90 Dunstable Road, Luton LU1 1EH

New Way, www.newway.org.uk

Prodigal Project, www.prodigal-project.com

Sarum College, www.sarum.ac.uk

Urban Theology Unit, www.utusheffield.fsnet.co.uk

There is an Association of Building Bridges Churches (ABC), comprising those involved in the previous stage of BBH, which offers support and networking to local churches. See Key contacts, Appendix 3.

Appendix 3

Key contacts

The CCOM/CTBI development consultant for BBH Stage C

Revd Terry Tennens (Britain and Ireland)
Pepper House, Hall Road, Mount Bures, Colchester, CO8 5AS
tel. 01787 227 979; e-mail: terry.tennens@tesco.net

Scotland contact

Mr Brian Burden, tel. 01575 575280
e-mail: bburden@iname.com

Wales contact

Revd Siôn Aled Owen, tel. 01978 354448
e-mail: saocytun@prifardd.fsnet.co.uk

Ireland contact

Dr David Stevens, tel. 028 90663145
e-mail: icpep@email.com

The local Association of Building Churches (ABC)

Revd John Summers, ABC, Box Cottage, Aish, South Brent, South Devon TQ10 9JH; tel. 01364 72976; e-mail: JohnFelicity @summersbox.freeserve.co.uk

For policy questions *only*, write to Mr Simon Barrow, Secretary, CTBI Churches' Commission on Mission (bbh@ctbi.org.uk). For further contact details, and other networks concerned with similar issues, see web page, www.ctbi.org.uk/bbh.

Appendix 4

Bibliography

David Hay and Kate Hunt, *Understanding the Spirituality of People who Don't Go to Church*, University of Nottingham, 2000.

Jeanne Hinton, *Small and in Place: Practical Steps in Forming Small Christian Communities*, New Way Publications, n.d.

Mission Theological Advisory Group, *The Search for Faith and the Witness of the Church*, Church House Publishing, 1996.

Ann Morisy, *Beyond the Good Samaritan*, Mowbray, 1997.

Robert Warren, *Building Missionary Congregations*, Church House Publishing, 1995.